DISCARDED

Chinese Treasures from the Avery Brundage Collection

Asia House Gallery, New York • January 18–March 3, 1968
Detroit Institute of Arts • March 26–May 7, 1968
The Art Institute of Chicago • June 5–July 7, 1968
Honolulu Academy of Arts • August 1–September 15, 1968
Seattle Art Museum • October 15–December 1, 1968
Portland Art Museum • December 12–December 27, 1968
M. H. De Young Memorial Museum, San Francisco • January 15–February 16, 1969

(Overleaf: 100. Seated Buddha, Gilt Bronze, H. 15½ in. Posterior Chao Dynasty, dated 338 A.D.)

Chinese Treasures from the Avery Brundage Collection

René-Yvon Lefebvre d'Argencé

The Asia Society, Inc.

Distributed by New York Graphic Society Ltd.

CARL A. RUDISILL LIBRARY
LENOIR RHYNE COLLEGE

709.51
L52c
83202
May 1973

Chinese Treasures from the Avery Brundage Collection is the catalogue of an exhibition selected from the Collection by René-Yvon Lefebvre d'Argencé, Director, Avery Brundage Foundation, and shown in the Asia House Gallery in the winter of 1968 as an activity of The Asia Society, to further greater understanding between the United States and the peoples of Asia.

An Asia House Gallery Publication
Copyright 1968 by The Asia Society, Inc.
Printed in the United States of America
Library of Congress Catalogue Card Number: 68-12222

Contents

Acknowledgements

Since approximately half the objects in the Avery Brundage Collection of Asian Art are of Chinese origin, it seems logical that the first traveling exhibition should be confined to that section. As a matter of fact the Collection was started following an extended visit to the great Chinese exhibition in Burlington House, London, in 1935–1936.

Some of the pieces are very small, some quite large, some virtually unknown, some already world famous, but all, modest or spectacular, were selected personally as revealing some facet of a remarkable civilization.

To all those who have organized this exhibition, and more particularly Mr. Washburn in New York, Mr. Woods in Detroit, Mr. Sewell in Chicago, Mr. Fuller in Seattle, Mr. Foster in Honolulu, and Mr. d'Argencé and his staff in San Francisco, my thanks and appreciation.

Avery Brundage

Avery Brundage, the renowned Chicago financier and Olympic sports official, has collected both Oriental and Occidental art for over thirty years. His Asian collection of almost seven thousand pieces is unquestionably one of the most important that has been gathered by any individual in the West. Elsewhere than in America, in our time, nothing more unlikely than the formation of such a collection can be imagined. In a Communist country, it would have been impossible. We must understand it, perhaps, as itself a special kind of creation, one that was achievable only in our particular time and place. Dependent though it is upon large private resources, such collecting as this is even more dependent upon a strong human vision and on a truly indomitable will. Its assemblage represents a personal act of affirmation: it is a declaration of Avery Brundage's great faith in man and in the significance of man's history. Thus it may be understood as his own prodigious way of saying "yes" within that vast silence into which we are born and that each of us may break in his own way.

Historians have already clustered about this rich gathering of documents. As a mountain is to a climber, so is the past to a historian. Because the past is there, it must be visited. In league with these historians, such a collector as Mr. Brundage seeks to assemble the needful evidence, those diverse arts and artifacts that can partially reveal the conformations of earlier societies and times. But such things do not quickly render up their meaning and it may therefore be foreseen that the Avery Brundage Collection will supply generations of scholars with their elusive indications of the nature of certain human cultures that are now extinct.

We, as proud borrowers, take much pleasure in being able to display some of these documents. We are enabled to do this through the courtesy of Avery Brundage and his Foundation and through the kindness of the M. H. De Young Memorial Museum, in whose Asian Art Wing the collection is housed. We are most profoundly indebted to René-Yvon d'Argencé, Director of the Avery Brundage Foundation, whose careful and expert selection of the one hundred and seventeen objects in the exhibition will provide the first opportunity for many art lovers to view some of the finest works of art that Mr. Brundage has assembled. Mr. d'Argencé has assisted us in every detail of the undertaking. For five color plates we are thankful to *Apollo* magazine and to its kind editor, Mr. Denys Sutton.

Gordon B. Washburn
Director
Asia House Gallery

Introduction

The Avery Brundage Collection encompasses works of art from various parts of Europe, Africa, and South America, as well as from nearly the whole of Asia—an area extending from the Dardanelles to Tokyo and from Outer Mongolia to Java. Within the latter continent, the culture of China comes first with approximately thirty-five hundred items illustrating some forty-five hundred years of artistic achievement. A good half of the Brundage Collection, taken as a whole, is Chinese. This is not only the most numerous department of the Collection, it is also the most diversified. Whereas for other cultures Avery Brundage has sometimes concentrated on a few major branches of their artistic expression, as for instance with the pottery of Persia and the sculpture of India, he has explored all facets of Chinese art. One reason for this unusual curiosity—almost a fascination—is that in the course of his extensive studies and travels Mr. Brundage was to become acutely responsive to the universality of the Chinese esthetic approach. He responded equally, moreover, to the magic of the Chinese hand, which had excelled over the centuries in so many media, including several, such as jade, lacquer, and porcelain, that were then unknown to the rest of the world. He also realized very early that, so far as China is concerned, our usual Western distinctions between major and minor arts and all similar pigeon-holes are often artificial barriers which should be relegated to the rank of teaching devices.

Even our term "visual arts" does not very perfectly fit within a Chinese context, the only important exceptions being calligraphies, paintings—which are frequently intellectual exercises as much as esthetic experiments—and the chinoiseries of the later periods. As a rule, whether we speak of ancient Chinese bronzes, ceramics, jades, lacquers, or sculptures, Chinese *objets d'art* are really objects made for very concrete and specific purposes. They were not created merely to be looked at but also to be handled. They call for a tactile as much as a visual appreciation and it is unfortunate that such a practice cannot be encouraged in public museums. One of the marvels of the Chinese way of life is that so much work, skill, love, and imagination went into the manufacture of objects for daily use. It is another marvel that, even when divorced from their original environment and deprived of their tactile appeal, they still lend themselves to the enthusiastic appreciation of modern Western eyes.

•

The largest section of the Chinese department of the Brundage Collection is that of its ceramics, which number approximately fifteen hundred items ranging from painted potteries dating from the Neolithic period (No. 53) to the colorful and sometimes over-ornate porcelains of the last reigns of the Ch'ing dynasty (No. 93). Indeed, the material is so extensive and so diversified that it could serve to illustrate a detailed history of Chinese ceramics throughout the ages. Each main step in the evolution of taste and technique is clearly marked by at least a few outstanding specimens. Yet whether in this field or in others, it was never Avery Brundage's ideal merely to build up a study collection wherein all phases of the Chinese ceramic production should be equally represented, their value depending on their technical and historical significance. Always reaching beyond technical and historical factors, his day-to-day choice and ultimately the overall composition of the collection were determined by his own taste. This personal taste is best reflected in the preponderance of such groups as T'ang three-color figurines (No. 64), Sung monochromes (Nos. 69, 70, 74, 75, 76), celadons of all periods from the third to the eighteenth century (Nos. 60, 61, 68, 69, 91), and multi-colored wares of the Ming and Ch'ing dynasties (Nos. 84, 85, 86, 88, 93) including an unusually large group of Swatow wares.

Even a casual glance at the items that have been selected for this exhibition will reveal that in ceramics as well as in other branches of Chinese art, downright realism and uncompromising abstraction are comparatively rare. One reason for this is that, with the exception of relatively short periods of time, the Chinese artist, whether a painter, calligrapher, jade carver, bronze caster, lacquerer, or ceramist, was indeed a man with a message—but a message that should be accessible to the community whose historical heritage and religious beliefs he fully shared. Thus, the Chinese artist addressed himself, as a rule, to the souls as well as to the senses of his contemporaries. This is best revealed in his choice of decorative motifs, which are usually adapted to a historical or religious context and are, in consequence, essentially symbolic in character.

In the Neolithic, Shang, and early Chou times practically all the important symbols were derived from common animal shapes: birds, fish, or insects. They even included dragons or *t'ao-t'ieh* masks. But in subsequent periods "the Chinese pantheon became so multitudinous that there is scarcely a being or a thing which has not been at some time or other, propitiated, worshipped" and consequently used as a decorative motif. In his book *Outlines of Chinese Symbolism and Art Motives,* from which the above quotation has been extracted, C. A. S. Williams has listed one thousand entries ranging from Ant, Bat, and Castanets, to Vermicelli, Witch-dancers, and Zodiac. Basically, all symbolic motifs can be traced to four main sources: mythology, religious beliefs (i.e. ancestor worship, Confucianism, Taoism, and Buddhism), history, and associations of ideas. The last source deserves a special mention because it generally escapes the notice of non-Chinese people. The Chinese are very fond of playing upon words and, with a language known for its wealth in homophones, they have become the most proficient punsters in the world. A number of puns have been codified and are constantly used in the decoration of art objects. For instance, the word for happiness is *fu*, and so is the word for bat. Traditionally there are Five Happinesses: Old Age, Wealth, Health, Love of Virtue, and Natural Death—hence the use of five bats as a standard decorative motif. Similarly, the fish became a symbol of wealth or abundance because the word for fish and for superfluity are homophones (No. 85). Comparable associations of ideas can also be grounded in the system of writing. In Chinese, "Happiness" is written with a single character. When this character is doubled to form an indivisible whole, it automatically becomes "Double Happiness" and stands as an ideal decorative motif for gifts to be offered to young couples.

•

The second largest section of the Chinese collection is that of Jades, with over one thousand items illustrating this lapidary art from its neolithic origins to modern times. Although jade—whether nephrite or jadeite—was never found in China proper in noticeable quantities, very early it became the Chinese gem par excellence. Indeed, it is the only precious stone to which the Chinese paid enduring respect, probably because it was the only one capable of satisfying their tactile as well as their visual sense. Although extremely compact, tough, and hard, jade is very soft to the hand. Cool when left alone, in contact with body temperature it grows warm very quickly. It catches light rays with brilliance but also with an intense, watery warmth. There is something definitely sensuous about jade and to ignore this aspect of the material is to ignore a whole segment of the traditional Chinese way of life which owes so much to a warm and human epicureanism.

Here, again, some periods or groups of material are better or more strongly represented than others. Such are the jades of the Warring States period (Nos. 40–42) and of the eighteenth century (Nos. 49–52) which are widely accepted as the peaks of Chinese lapidary art. This section also contains an unusually large and diversified display of animal figurines, among them many belonging to the still ill-defined medieval periods.

Even the small selection of jades in this exhibition sheds some light on a thematic development, not only of this medium but of Chinese art in general. This development can be described as a slow and gradual conquest of the universe—a conquest which was achieved in three main, successive waves. The earliest periods focused on the most vital elements in man's environment. Shang and early Chou art was essentially an animal art. Even deities themselves were conceived of as super-animals or animals endowed with supernatural powers, or they actively symbolized supernatural forces. Man, as subject matter, played a meager role in Shang and early Chou art. Whether in jade, bronze, or ceramics, human representations are very rare. When they do occur, they lack individuality and appear as passive mirrors reflecting the face—a face not of any given person but of mankind, past, present, and future (Nos. 1, 26).

The late Chou and Han periods are a turning point and mark the beginning of the second stage of the conquest. This is the time when man assumes a central position which he will retain for about twelve hundred years, until the end of the T'ang dynasty. As seen in Han art, man is essentially a social creature. Han imagery provides the student with a cross-section of society, and one that is fully detailed. Both sexes, all ages, all professions or typical activities such as hunting, fishing, farming, etc., are represented (Nos. 21, 57, 59).

During the Six Dynasties, there was a shift of emphasis due mainly to the propagation of Buddhism. Man became a contemplative or religious subject, frequently shown in the attitude of prayer, or taking part in processions and other religious ceremonies. Conversely, for the first time in China, deities take on a wholly anthropomorphic appearance. In Buddhist art the pantheon is wholly humanized and, just as might be expected, this is the period of Chinese art which is most directly accessible to Westerners (Nos. 100–112).

The third and final wave of this conquest of the universe became manifest during the tenth century and reached its apex in the eighteenth century. It corresponded to the increasing importance given by Chinese artists to natural settings (Nos. 49, 50, 52, 114, 115, 117). It has been said that man in China was ultimately displaced by nature, and the promoters of this theory usually point to the smallness of the human figure in mature landscape painting (Nos. 114, 117). In effect, nature did not displace man any more than man had displaced animals. From the Shang period on, the general trend was toward an increasingly broader artistic vision, each phase building on the previous one with remarkably little elimination. If human figures are tiny in classical landscape painting, it is not because man was belittled or because nature was dehumanized, but simply because the conquest was completed. The whole universe had entered the artist's vision and quite naturally man fell into place—he was simply drawn to scale in his proper place between heaven and earth.

•

Numerically, bronzes occupy the third rank in the Chinese department of the Collection. Of more than six hundred items there are nearly two hundred fifty ancient vessels, representing all the major Shang and Chou types, as well as about ninety mirrors ranging in time from the Warring States to the Sung period (Nos. 28, 31–34). The remaining items include bells, weapons, chariot fittings, belt-hooks, and other artifacts illustrating the various periods and styles of China's Bronze Age. This section is not only well-balanced and replete with specimens of the highest artistic quality, it also contains numerous objects that cannot be found in other collections.

As has already been stated elsewhere, one of the most important aspects of the stylistic development of the ancient bronze art of China is that of its dynamic order. From Shang to Western Chou, Ch'un-ch'iu, and Warring States one can follow, step by step, the birth, emergence, and blossoming of a powerful calligraphic rhythm. It would seem that by the end of the Warring States the notion that life, motion, and line are inseparable entities was firmly established. From that time on, and perhaps from even earlier, Chinese artists conceived of life as a kind of spiritual energy which cannot be divorced from its material support. In practice this meant that matter (or shape) must be energized—a condition which can be achieved only through a suggestion of motion or movement. This motion cannot be a superficial one. It cannot be a muscular motion. It must be a reflection of the all-pervading pulse of nature. It must be the primary manifestation of life. One can easily imagine a great variety of plastic, graphic, or even chromatic means whereby a sculptor, calligrapher, or painter might try to suggest motion, and through motion that life-giving harmony which in China was essential to all works of art. Chinese artists have tried them all in various degrees, but the predominant and most enduring method has been the linear approach, whereby the line itself becomes the ideal motion-bearing and, in consequence, life-bearing vehicle.

This linear approach was not merely logical—it was conditioned to a large extent by a unique system of writing and by the tremendously demanding training that was required to master it. Most creative artists spent many of the formative years of their lives training their brains, eyes, and hands to transcribe all things and concepts in the universe in terms of images made of lines arranged in rhythmical compositions. It stands to reason that they would ultimately become indifferent to any reality that could not be expressed in terms of rhythmical lines. This is why calligraphy, at a very early date, came to be regarded as the highest art form. It was the only means capable of conveying simultaneously the totality of Chinese esthetic ideals. It was the only form wherein the trinity of life, motion, and line could be found in immediate and completely unadulterated form.

•

The next section of the Brundage Collection, in order of numerical importance, comprises some two hundred pieces of lacquer, cloisonné, enameled ware, rhinoceros horn, tortoise shell, glass, cloth, gold, silver, and various precious or semi-precious stones. All these categories are grouped here for the sake of convenience and also because they belong mostly to the Ming and Ch'ing periods, wherein this type of material can be regarded as essentially decorative. As Sir Harry Garner points out, early lacquers of the Warring States and Han periods (Nos. 94, 95) are a special case. He has written that "during this period we see the birth of new ideas in the abstract delineation of landscape, and it is in the lacquers that these ideas are developed with the greatest skill in association with brushwork of great vitality."

•

From the fourth century A.D. to the middle of the ninth century, the most striking novelties and also some of the most remarkable artistic achievements are to be found in the field of sculpture. Needless to say, there were sculptors in China before the fourth century and after the ninth, but on the whole their contribution has remained somewhat minimal. This exceptional sculptural trend was hardly the fruit of an internal evolution. It was provoked and continuously nourished by a foreign religious and cultural force, that of Buddhism. This is well reflected in the sculpture collection. Its two hundred components are overwhelmingly of Buddhist inspiration. They can be marshalled into two main categories, bronzes and stones. The gilded bronzes and many of the stones illustrate styles prevailing in the famous cave-temples of Yün-kang, Lung-men, T'ien-lung shan, and Hsiang-t'ang shan (Nos. 108, 109). The unusually rich examples of gilt bronze statuettes, shrines, and altar pieces show the gradual evolution of Buddhist concepts and visions from the fourth to the eighteenth century. (A large group of subjects of Tibetan inspiration could not be shown here.)

•

The least developed section of the Collection is that of paintings, a field of collecting in which Avery Brundage has been active only in recent years. One might be tempted to state that he has so far shown a marked predilection for what is known as the Southern School of Chinese painting except that our possessions are still too few to permit any kind of generalization. All that can be said is that Mr. Brundage reacts in very much the same manner as did the famous late Ming critics who codified painting styles into "Northern or Southern Schools." Arbitrary and controversial as it may be, this approach also reflects another basic factor in the Chinese way of life and artistic production, that of regionalism. In our highly mechanized civilization, jet planes and mass media have practically abolished barriers of geography and time. Due to a constant interchange of population and ideas, regionalism now tends to be reduced to a difference in climate and to a few quaint and disintegrating local traditions to be studied as if they were so many museum pieces. The main trend is toward uniformity, and quite naturally this uniformity extends to cultural and artistic activities. In contrast, traditional China was anything but homogeneous. From one province to another or even from one part of a province to another, people had a different physical appearance, spoke different dialects, wore different types of dress, ate different types of food, lived in widely different environments and, very naturally, developed regional tastes, techniques, and even schools of art. Terms which recur constantly in contemporary Chinese literature, such as Shu silk and lacquer, Yüeh ceramics, or the Che and Wu schools of painting, are a good case in point. They refer to partly political, partly ethnic divisions of the land—which had been established as early as the third century B.C. Culturally speaking, it can be said that southern China lagged behind northern China until approximately the downfall of the Han dynasty. From the third to the eleventh century (which was marked by the advent of the Southern Sung period) a balance was established. Thereafter the south was frequently ahead of the north, at least in such fields as painting and ceramics.

The present selection truly reflects the actual contents of the Brundage Collection. However, our choice is based neither on proportional statistics nor on merely intrinsic values. We accepted the premise that various groups should be represented in a balanced manner relative to their significance in comparison with other collections of similar nature. The only exceptions were made in the categories of monumental stone and wood sculptures, which could not be included in a traveling exhibition.

Previous choices made by Sir Harry Garner, Laurence Sickman, and Alexander Soper have served as precious guide-lines. So have the written comments of John Pope and Jan Fontein and the verbal ones offered by many scholars who attended the memorable "Brundage Symposium".

I am particularly grateful to Gordon Washburn and Virginia Field in New York, and to Clarence Shangraw, Yoshiko Kakudo, and Huang Woan-jen in San Francisco for their kind advice and indefatigable support.

René-Yvon Lefebvre d'Argencé
Director
Avery Brundage Foundation

Ritual Bronzes

1 Li-Ho. Middle Shang.
Erh-li-kang style. 15th–13th century B.C.
Bronze. H. 9 in., Diam. 6 in. B60B53.

This tripod for sacrificial wine has tall, hollow legs with pointed extremities, a dome-like top, a long, cone-shaped spout, and a flat handle cast in two parts. The top suggests a human mask with two bulging eyes; the spout and a wide aperture serve as the nose and mouth. A horizontal band on the neck is decorated with three panels in raised lines. Each panel, framed by rows of dots between parallel bow strings, contains an elongated and abstracted *t'ao-t'ieh* mask. The walls of the vessel are thin and smooth, the patina is gray-green. There are several traces of imperfect casting.

2 Ho. Late Shang. *(upper left)*
13th–11th century B.C.
Bronze. H. 7¾ in., Diam. 5½ in. B60B995.

Believed to be the only one of its kind in existence, this ceremonial wine vessel has a cylindrical body with constricted neck and foot, and a dome-shaped cover surmounted by a circular knob with everted rim. The tubular, slightly tapering spout juts out from the shoulder and the lower part of the neck. A long, sturdy handle spans almost the entire length of the belly; the upper part of this handle consists of a bovine head without lower jaw. In addition to two lug handles, the neck is equipped with a loop. Originally, a chain connected this loop with a similar one on the lid. The belly is plain but the cover, neck, and foot are decorated with gaping and turning dragons set against a meander background. The spout is incised with four rising blades and a band of barbed spirals. The zones of decoration bear traces of a red filling and the patina is unusually rich, with patches of azurite and malachite. A large piece of burial cloth has become an integral part of the patination. A two-character inscription is half concealed by the handle, and the same inscription was cast inside the lid.

Published: B. Karlgren, *BMFEA*, No. 21 (1949), Pl. 12: 2; Jung K., *Shang and Chou Bronzes*, Vol. 2 (1941), Pl. 644; R-Y. Lefebvre d'Argencé, *A.B.C. Bronzes*, Pl. VII.

(Key to abbreviations appears on page 148.)

3 Li-Ting. Late Shang. *(lower left)*
An-yang style. 1300–1028 B.C.
Bronze. H. 8 in., Diam. 8 in. B60B1030.

This ceremonial food vessel stands on three solid and slightly splaying legs. The three lobes on the body fuse into each other to form a short neck. Two sturdy loop handles are attached to the everted mouth rim. The neck band is decorated with twelve whorl circles alternating with as many squares and crescents. On each lobe there is a large monster's mask of the bovine type. All these motifs stand out in relief against a background of rounded spirals. The whole surface is covered with a smooth grayish patina with traces of black filling. A vertical, four-character inscription in two rows is cast inside the vessel.

Published: d'Argencé, *A.B.C. Bronzes*, Pl. III; d'Argencé, *Apollo*, p. 115, Pl. X.

4 Chia. Later part of Late Shang. *(lower right)*
12th–11th century B.C.
Bronze. H. 11 in., Diam. 7½ in. B60B1019.

A sacrificial wine vessel, this *Chia* has a rounded, bulging body with an S-shaped profile and bulky, hollow, splayed legs that are triangular in cross section. The flaring rim is surmounted by rectangular uprights with caps in the shape of inverted beakers. The upper part of the massive, grooved handle bears a bovine head. The flat, circular lid is topped by a pair of free-sculptured, crested birds placed back to back. The main ornamental schemes are: a narrow belt of four-eyed motifs, triangles, and spirals on the lid; seventeen rising blades on the lip zone; *t'ao-t'ieh* shields and trunked dragons on the neck zone; large *t'ao-t'ieh* masks and small crested birds on the main body zone. The outer faces of the legs are decorated with *t'ao-t'ieh* hanging blades. There is a one-character inscription cast on the bottom of the vessel, whose surface is covered with a smooth, olive-brown patina with secondary incrustations.

Published: d'Argencé, *A.B.C. Bronzes*, Pl. XIII.

Ritual Bronzes

5 **Yu.** Late Shang. *(upper left)*
13th–11th century B.C.
Bronze. H. 14¾ in., Diam. 6¾ in. B60B1008.

This bottle-shaped container, a *Yu,* is classified as a vessel for sacrificial wine. The large, flanged, and bow-shaped handle terminates in bovine masks with fangs. A dome-shaped cover is topped by a bird, in the round, standing on a short pillar. One side of the handle is connected to this pillar by means of an elaborate device consisting of two rings, a free-sculptured cicada, and a dragon biting its tail. The vessel is covered with finely incised *t'ao-t'ieh* masks, dragons, and spiral bands, arranged in four main zones of décor. The patina is a rich yellow with many brown patches.

Published: Karlgren, *BMFEA,* No. 34 (1962), Pl. 56-a; d'Argencé, *A.B.C. Bronzes,* Pl. XVI.

6 **Chih.** Later part of Late Shang. *(upper right)*
An-yang style. 12th–11th century B.C.
Bronze. H. 7½ in., W. 5 in. B60B3+.

This goblet-shaped container is traditionally classified as a vessel for drinking ceremonial wine. Its S-shaped contours are emphasized by notched flanges. The body has two main zones of décor, each bearing a large owl with split body and protruding mask set against a meander background. Trunked dragons can be seen above, behind, and below the wings of the birds and a *t'ao-t'ieh* mask occupies a rectangular area between their legs. On the lid are four gaping dragons and four small birds in profile. The vessel is inscribed. Its surface is covered with a smooth, light green patina with traces of red filling.

Published: d'Argencé, *A.B.C. Bronzes,* Pl. XVIII:A; d'Argencé, *Apollo,* p. 117, Fig. 6.

7 **Fang I.** Late Shang. *(lower left)*
13th–11th century B.C.
Bronze. H. 7½ in., W. 4 in. B60B997.

A square vessel for ceremonial wine, this *Fang I* has a roof-shaped cover and a hollow base with four large, semicircular notches. Each side is framed by flat, narrow, scored strips. There are large *t'ao-t'ieh* masks on the cover and on the central panels of the body; the upper body zone and the foot zone show two types of dragons. These varied motifs stand out in relief against a meander background. The surface is covered with a rich, variegated patina with traces of red filling.

Published: d'Argencé, *A.B.C. Bronzes,* Pl. XII:A.

8 **Ku.** Late Shang. *(lower right)*
An-yang style. 1300–1028 B.C.
Bronze. H. 11¾ in., W. 6¼ in. B60B777.

This *Ku,* a chalice-like container for drinking ceremonial wine, has a central bulging part and a flaring hollow base. There are four perforations at the base of the central zone. Notched flanges emphasize the contours of the lower part of the vessel, which is covered with finely incised motifs on the trumpet, *t'ao-t'ieh* masks on the central and foot zones, snakes and cicadae on the narrow intermediary belts. A grayish-green patina shows traces of azurite and malachite. There is a one-character inscription cast inside the foot.

Published: d'Argencé, *A.B.C. Bronzes,* Pl. X.

Ritual Bronzes

9 **Tsun.** Later part of Late Shang.
Ca. 11th century B.C.
Bronze. H. 9 in., L. 13 in. B60B1+.

The surface of this ceremonial wine vessel in the shape of a rhinoceros is quite plain except for ridges behind the ears and the shoulders, and a series of grooves on either side of the lower lip. These ridges and grooves suggest folds of skin. Hooves are also clearly delineated. The lid, now missing, was probably dome-shaped. The smooth brownish-black patina is pitted with grayish-green and red patches, producing a grumous effect. An inscription of twenty-seven characters cast on the bottom of the vessel refers to a gift of cowries made by the king to a high official on the occasion of a sacrifice commemorating a successful expedition.

Published: Kaizuka, S., *Sekai Bunkashi Taikei*, Vol. 15 (1958), Pl. 10; A. G. Wenley, *Archives of the Chinese Art Society of America*, Vol. VI (1952), Frontis.; L. Sickman and A. Soper, *The Art and Architecture of China*, Baltimore, 1960, Pl. IV; S. Mizuno, *Bronzes and Jades of Ancient China*, Japan, 1959, Pls. 70, 71; E. Consten, *Das Alte China*, Stuttgart, 1958, Pl. 34; W. Watson, *Ancient Chinese Bronzes*, London, 1962, Pl. 25a; d'Argencé, *A.B.C. Bronzes,* Pl. XIX and cover; d'Argencé, *Apollo*, p. 118, Pl. XI; d'Argencé, *Asia Foundation*, Pl. III.

10 **Chüeh.** Later part of Late Shang.
12th–11th century B.C.
Bronze. H. 9¼ in., W. 7¾ in. B60B1049.

This unusual sacrificial wine vessel stands on three slender, splayed legs with sharp extremities. Its mouth opens into a channel-like spout on one side and a pointed "tail" on the other. The mouth supports two vertical uprights with caps in the shape of coiling snakes. The front part of the lid shows a bovine head in the round; a reduced and simplified variant of this head forms the upper part of the handle. The surface decoration, heavily corroded, consists of animal shapes in low relief against a meander background—dragons on the lid and belly, cicadae of different types under the spout and behind the handle, blades on the neck and legs. A ten-character inscription is cast inside the body and on the verso of the lid.

Published: Jung, *Shang and Chou Bronzes*, Peking (1941), Vol. 2, Fig. 430 (rubbing); d'Argencé, *A.B.C. Bronzes*, Pl. IX.

11 Kuang. Later part of Late Shang. *(upper right)*
12th–11th century B.C.
Bronze. H. 9 in., W. 9 in. B60B1032.

The contours of the tripartite, boat-shaped body are emphasized by wide flanges with scores and spurs. The handle represents the head of a ram holding a bird in its mouth. A large bovine head with bottle-shaped horns, thick lips, and bared teeth forms the front part of the massive lid. The rear of the vessel terminates in a spur-like handle, which is also the beak of a "birdicized" *t'ao-t'ieh* mask with dragon-shaped horns. The surface of the *Kuang* is covered with a profusion of animal shapes, ranging from large *t'ao-t'ieh* masks on the central zone to diminutive elephants and hares on the neck and lid. These motifs stand out in relief against a background of minute meanders. The ornament is unusually sharp, and the light green patina contains vividly contrasting incrustations of cuprite and malachite, as well as traces of red filling.

Published: d'Argencé, *A.B.C. Bronzes*, Pl. XX; d'Argencé, *Apollo*, p. 118, Pl. XII.

12 Fang Ting. Early Western Chou. *(lower left)*
Ca. 1024–1005 B.C.
Bronze. H. 10 in., W. 9 in. B60B2+.

This vessel for sacrificial food, a square *Ting*, is supported by four legs in the shape of long-beaked birds. Two large, loop handles rise vertically from the narrow ends of the rim. Each side of the body is divided into two panels by sturdy, hooked flanges. Each panel contains a bird in profile, in high relief against a meander background. At each corner the beaks of two birds join to form shoe-shaped projections. The surface is covered by rich, green patination with traces of black filling. A thirty-three character inscription, cast inside one of the long walls and part of the bottom, records an event that took place in the first years of the Chou dynasty. This vessel is said to have been unearthed in 1924 from a royal tomb in Shensi province.

Published: Ch'en Meng-chia, "Chronology of Bronze Vessels of the Western Chou," *Kaogu Xuebao*, No. 9 (1955), Pl. 9, and No. 10 (1956), Pl. 4; L. Sickman, *Selections from the Avery Brundage Collection*, San Francisco, 1960, No. 5; Consten, *Das Alte China*, Pl. 30; d'Argencé, *Asia Foundation*, Pl. VII; d'Argencé, *Apollo*, p. 121, Fig. 10.

13 Yi. Mid Western Chou. *(lower right)*
10th–9th century B.C.
Bronze. H. 6 in., W. 11 in. B60B1027.

A vessel for sacrificial water, this semi-zoomorphic *Yi* stands on four short, gnarled legs. The container is in the shape of a sauce boat and ends in an elongated channel-like spout. The upper part of the bow-shaped handle is a feline head in the round. A wide band of dragon heads, with protruding eyes and intertwining necks and crests, encircles the body. These motifs stand in relief against a loose background of meanders in raised lines. The vessel is covered with light green patination with secondary incrustations.

Published: d'Argencé, *A.B.C. Bronzes*, Pl. XXXIV:A; d'Argencé, *Apollo*, p. 122, Fig. 12.

14 **Hu.** Mid Western Chou.
10th–9th century B.C.
Bronze. H. 14½ in., W. 7 in. B60B1054.

A bottle-shaped vessel with flattened sides, this *Hu* was used in connection with the offering of sacrificial wine. The dome-shaped lid is topped by a tubular knob, and two rings, originally connected with a chain handle, appear on the shoulder. Tiers of scale motifs encircle the lid and the neck. The body is divided into eight panels by intersecting, plain bands which suggest leather strappings. Each panel is filled by a large bird in profile. The heavily encrusted surface is covered with a green patina. There is a two-character inscription cast in raised lines inside the lid.

Published: *Sekai Kōkogaku Taikei*, Vol. 6, Pl. 135; d'Argencé, *A.B.C. Bronzes*, Pl. XXXIII:A; d'Argencé, *Apollo,* p. 122, Fig. 11.

Ritual Bronzes

15 **Hu.** Late Western Chou. *(upper left)*
9th–8th century B.C.
Bronze. H. 13½ in., W. 10 in. B60B1012.

This pear-shaped vessel with flattened sides, a *Hu*, was used as a container for sacrificial wine. The openwork crown of the mouth encloses a reclining bull in the round. The elaborate handles consist of sturdy loops topped by monsters' masks whose trunks are in the shape of long-necked, crested, and fanged dragons. The loops also hold large, loose rings, oval in section and incised with three concentric circles on the outside. The body of the vessel is divided into four zones of decoration. Rising blades and spiraling animal shapes appear on the neck and shoulder. On the belly an enlarged and dissolved version of similar animal shapes is enclosed in a network of bands in flat relief, with triangular or conical projections at the points of intersection. The surface is covered with a dark-and-light-green patina. The vessel bears scratched inscriptions in three different places: on the lid, the mouth, and the neck.

Published: J. D. La Plante, *Arts of the Chou Dynasty*, Stanford, California, 1958, No. 53; *Sekai Kōkogaku Taikei*, Vol. 6, Fig. 136; d'Argencé, *A.B.C. Bronzes*, Pl. XXXV:A; d'Argencé, *Asia Foundation*, Fig. 7.

16 **Lei.** Late Ch'un-ch'iu or Early Warring States.
7th–5th century B.C. *(lower right)*
Bronze. H. 12¼ in., W. 11 in. B60B1009.

This unusual vessel for ceremonial wine, a *Lei*, has the contours of a bulging jar with a flat bottom. It has two sets of handles; the small rings were originally connected with a chain, the large rings hang from the "noses" of monsters' masks which were cast separately. Three main ornamental belts encircling the neck, shoulder, and belly show variants of spiraling and intertwining snake-like shapes. The two monsters' masks on the shoulder are also made of small snakes and snakes' scales. The surface of the vessel is covered with a smooth, light green patina.

Published: d'Argencé, *A.B.C. Bronzes*, Pl. XXXVIII.

17 **Hu.** Mid Warring States.
5th–4th century B.C.
Bronze. H. 18¼ in., Diam. 9⅛ in. B60B974.

This tall, bottle-shaped vessel for sacrificial wine, a *Hu*, stands on a sturdy ring foot. It has a detachable and widely flaring mouth. Its handles are two felines in the round, their heads turned back over their shoulders. The body is divided into four large belts of decoration by narrow, raised bands showing incised geometric patterns. The four main scenes depict fantastic carrousels of hybrid creatures, chasing one another in no apparent order. These designs appear in intaglio. The uneven, grayish-green patina is heavily encrusted.

Published: d'Argencé, *A.B.C. Bronzes*, Pl. XLII:B.

18 **Yi.** Early Warring States. *(lower right)*
Li-yü style. Ca. 5th century B.C.
Bronze. H. 5⅜ in., L. 9¾ in. B65B65.

Unlike our previous example (see No. 13), this *Yi*, a vessel for sacrificial water, sits on a flat base encircled by a rope pattern in high relief. A similar "rope" circles the body near the upper edge, dipping under the spout which is partly covered with an unusual openwork plaque of intertwining snakes. A wide band on the body is filled with a meander background alternating with flat, plain, and somewhat dissolved spirals. The patina is grayish-green.

Published: Watson, *Ancient Chinese Bronzes*, Pl. 63a; d'Argencé, *A.B.C. Bronzes*, Pl. XLI; d'Argencé, *Apollo*, p. 124, Fig. 16.

19 **P'an.** Late Warring States. *(upper left)*
Chin-ts'un type. Ca. 3rd century B.C.
Bronze. H. 5 in., Diam. 3⅞ in. B66B23.

A circular tray is supported by three standing, fully-dressed human figures. Around the rim are attached twelve petal-like projections; each bears a bird's head in low relief. Four loops on the sides were originally connected by suspension chains. The outside is incised all around with geometric patterns. The corroded surface is covered with a brown, red, and green patina.

Published: La Plante, *Arts of the Chou Dynasty*, No. 53; B. Gyllensvärd, *BMFEA*, No. 34 (1962), Pl. VIII:C.

20 **Lien.** Warring States to Western Han. *(upper right)*
3rd–1st century B.C.
Gilt bronze. H. 11 in., W. 7¾ in. B60B953.

This cosmetic box, a *Lien*, is supported by three tiny, dancing bears with twisted bodies. The double-domed lid is surmounted by three phoenixes in the round and, at a lower level, three monsters' masks elevated on short pillars. On the box are two *t'ao-t'ieh* masks holding loose rings. Cloud-shaped volutes, spirals, and other geometric figures inlaid in silver enhance the gilded surface.

Published: d'Argencé, *A.B.C. Bronzes*, Pl. LIII:A.

21 **Lien.** Han. *(lower left)*
206 B.C.–A.D. 221.
Gilt bronze. H. 5 in., Diam. 6½ in. B60B951.

Three legs in the shape of bear figurines support this *Lien*. It has two handles consisting of phoenixes holding loose rings. The whole surface is covered with a relief design of twenty-seven figures—hunters, game, wild beasts, genii, and fabulous animals—in a setting of wavy mountains.

Published: d'Argencé, *A.B.C. Bronzes*, Pl. LIII:B.

Miscellaneous Bronzes

22 Linch-Pin. Late Shang.
13th–11th century B.C.
Bronze. H. 4 in. B60B832.

A realistic bull's head with flat horns surmounts this linch-pin. The extended ears, bulging eyes, and sensitive muzzle convey a feeling of intense alertness. The bronze has a bluish-green patination with silvery-gray iridescense.

Published: d'Argencé, *A.B.C. Bronzes*, Pl. XXX:A.

Miscellaneous Bronzes

23 **Ch'i-Ling.** Late Shang. *(lower left)*
13th–11th century B.C.
Bronze. L. 12½ in. B60B826.

This bow-shaped artifact, a chariot or harness fitting, has jingle-bells at either extremity. Its decorative motifs, birds and cicadae, set against a spiral filling, are enhanced by insets of turquoise. The smooth patination is gray-green with cuprite incrustations.

Published: d'Argencé, *A.B.C. Bronzes*, Pl. XXII:A.

24 **Yüeh.** Late Shang. *(upper right)*
13th–11th century B.C.
Bronze. H. 8 in., W. 5 in. B60B790.

A ceremonial axe, this *Yüeh* has an asymmetrical blade, and a rectangular tang placed slightly off center. The upper part of the tang is decorated with an animal shape in profile. The blade shows a coiling dragon with gaping mouth, large fangs, and scaled body. It has a rough green patination with secondary incrustations.

Published: d'Argencé, *A.B.C. Bronzes*, Pl. XIII.

Miscellaneous Bronzes

25 Horse's Head. Late Shang or Early Western Chou.
11th–10th century B.C.
Bronze. H. 3¾ in., L. 3¾ in. B60B833.

The head is rendered realistically except for barbed C-shapes on the cheeks and on either side of the nose ridge. There is a suspension or attachment loop under the chin. The patination is black with secondary incrustations.

Published: d'Argencé, *A.B.C. Bronzes*, Pl. XXV:A.

26 Ceremonial Blade. Late Western Chou.
9th–8th century B.C.
Bronze. H. 6¾ in. B60B1065.

The edge of this unusual weapon is formed by the back of a coiling dragon whose open mouth holds a flat-nosed human head with a protruding mouth and large, U-shaped ears. The inside of this head is hollow. Together with two rings attached to the lower part of the body of the dragon, it served to secure the shaft. A large, scaled snake is incised on either side of the inner part of the blade. The fixation rings bear scale motifs.

Miscellaneous Bronzes

27 **Chung.** Warring States.
5th–4th century B.C.
Bronze. H. 26 in., W. 12 in. B60S551.

This clapperless bell, a *Chung*, is oval in section and has a concave base line. Its solid, cylindrical handle is equipped with a reinforced suspension ring in the shape of a winged feline biting its tail. Three rows of nipples on the upper part of the *Chung* alternate with narrow belts bearing interlaced animal shapes in low relief. Similar shapes form three zones of decoration on the handle. On the lower part of the body a wide panel contains a large *t'ao-t'ieh* mask amidst a maze of dissolved and intertwining dragon and bird shapes, some of them rather realistic.

Published: La Plante, *Arts of the Chou Dynasty*, No. 98; d'Argencé, *A.B.C. Bronzes*, Pl. XLVI:A.

Miscellaneous Bronzes

28 Mirror. Warring States.
4th–3rd century B.C.
Bronze. Diam. 5¾ in. B60B559.

This thin, circular mirror with an elevated rim and fluted central knob bears a single large, ornamental band of axial quatrefoils and spiraling dragons in low relief. These motifs stand against a granulated background with geometrical schemes in thin raised line. The patina is smooth and black.

29 Chariot Fitting. Late Warring States.
Chin-ts'un style. Ca. 3rd century B.C.
Bronze with silver inlay. L. 8½ in. B60B702.

A thin-headed, long-necked and bodiless dragon serves as the handle of a hollow, rectangular casing for the insertion of a wooden piece. The dragon has large, protruding eyes and holds a bead in its beaked mouth. Starting from the neck of the dragon, there is an elaborate decoration of geometric designs inlaid in silver.

Published: d'Argencé, *A.B.C. Bronzes*, Pl. XLIX:B.

Miscellaneous Bronzes

30 Pair of Bear Caryatids. Western Han.
206 B.C.–A.D. 8.
Gilt bronze. H. 2½ in. B66B12, B66B13.

The animals are rendered realistically. Manes and hair are suggested by surface chasing. Ears, eyes, shoulders, knees, and belly are decorated with turquoise insets. The squatting beasts are hollow, with large apertures at top and bottom; the top aperture is semi-circular, the bottom one hexagonal. The legs of a piece of furniture were probably inserted into these holes.

Miscellaneous Bronzes

31 Mirror. Late Han. *(upper left)*
25–221 A.D.
Bronze. Diam. 8¼ in. B60B597.

This thick mirror of the "animal belt" type has a wide, elevated, outer band and a hemispherical knob. There are four main concentric zones of ornament: (1) around the knob, small nipples alternating with the seal characters of a dedicatory inscription; (2) band of barbed S-shaped spirals; (3) seven quatrefoils with central nipples alternating with various animals, monsters, and genii; (4) broad outer band with a variety of human and animal subjects including the animals of the four cardinal points—tortoise, tiger, bird, and dragon. The patination is a smooth grayish-black with light green incrustations.

32 Mirror. Early T'ang. *(lower left)*
Later part of 7th century A.D.
Bronze. Diam. 5⅞ in. B60B530.

Of thick bronze, this mirror has a hemispherical knob, an elevated rim, and a raised border in the central field. Three main concentric bands of ornament appear: (1) conventional floral scheme, suggesting an open corolla; (2) twelve animals of the zodiac, i.e., rat, ox, dog (instead of usual tiger), hare, dragon, snake, horse, sheep, monkey, cock, another type of dog, and boar; (3) border of scrolls of tendrils. It has a silvery patination with heavy incrustations.

33 Mirror. Mid T'ang. *(upper right)*
8th century A.D.
Bronze. Diam. 8⅞ in. B60B599.

An eight-lobed mirror with a small hemispherical knob has one zone of decoration, filled with a wildly contorted dragon and eight large, fungus-like clouds. The winged, scale-covered, thin-necked dragon has three-clawed jaws and forked antlers. A long, curling tongue projects from its gaping mouth. The bronze has a silvery patination with heavy incrustations.

34 Mirror. Mid T'ang. *(lower right)*
8th century A.D.
Bronze. Diam. 5½ in. B60B547.

This mirror has an elevated rim and a hemispherical knob. In axial position around the central knob are four floral sprays. The central field is adorned with a hunting scene including two archers, a lancer, and a man equipped with a lasso. All four men ride galloping horses and pursue two hares, a lion, and a boar. The outer border is decorated with seventeen fungus-like clouds. The patination is silvery, with some incrustations.

Jades

35 **Bird.** Neolithic.
Ca. 1500 B.C.
Jade. L. 3⅛ in., H. 2 in. B60J331.

This jade pebble is carved in the shape of a bird with rounded body and small head. Wings and legs are outlined by deep incisions and a shallow slit delineates the mouth. There are no indications of eyes or feet. The color is mottled grayish-green and yellowish.

Published: A. Salmony, *Chinese Jade*, New York, 1963, Pl. II:3; d'Argencé, *Asia Foundation*, Pl. II.

36 **Tiger Head.** Shang.
13th–11th century B.C.
Jade. L. 1⅛ in. B60J716.

A large *t'ao-t'ieh* mask in fairly high relief with open mouth, lower jaw, fangs, and two stump legs decorates this short cylinder which has a large vertical perforation. The jade is mottled, light green with brown and black markings, and the underside is calcified in parts.

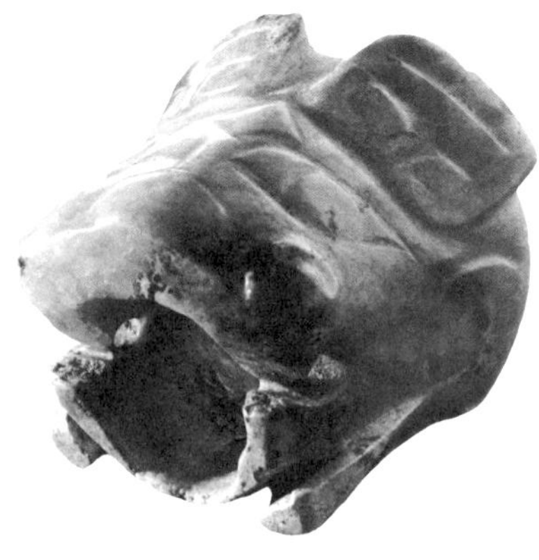

38 **Bird Pendant.** Early Western Chou. *(center right)*
Ca. 10th century B.C.
Jade. L. 1⅜ in. B60J632.

Both sides of this thin plaque show the profile of a cormorant in a crouching posture, with long, curving beak, and large, bulging eye in relief. The area where the body joins the tail and legs is marked by a deep longitudinal groove. No wings are indicated but incisions mark the parting of the tail and the feet. A suspension hole appears low on the breast. The jade is a speckled tan with some incrustations.

Published: d'Argencé, *Apollo*, p. 135, Fig. 1(c).

37 **Tiger Pendant.** Shang or Early Western Chou.
13th–10th century B.C. *(upper right)*
Jade. L. 2¾ in. B60J538.

The profile of a tiger appears on both faces of this thin slab. The large head has an open mouth and turned-up nose. Ears, jaws, and curling tail are free-sculptured. Details of the ear, and the eyes, claws, shoulders, and haunches are indicated by bevelled lines. Perforations exist in the mouth and tail. The jade is grayish-green with brown markings and traces of cinnabar remain.

39 **Salamander Pendant.** Western Chou.
10th–8th century B.C. *(lower right)*
Jade. L. 3¼ in. B62J33.

The salamander forms a compactly geometricized shape, convex on top and flat underneath. Head, forelegs, and tail are free-sculptured. The only surface details are two bulging eyes in high relief and incised feet. The sharp ending of the tail would indicate that it served as a cutting tool. There is a suspension hole high on the head; the perforation was made from both sides. The color is light tan with black markings.

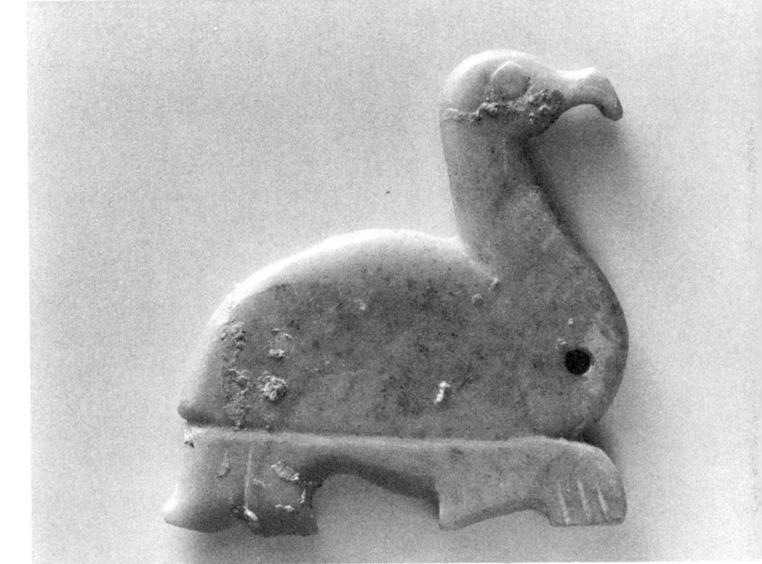

40 Tiger Pendant. Warring States.
Chin-ts'un style. Ca. 3rd century B.C.
Jade. L. 4⅜ in. B62J63.

This arc-shaped slab shows identical ornamental schemes on both sides. The body terminates in two addorsed tiger heads with pointed noses and beards, slit mouths, and elongated, pointed ears. Eyes, cheeks, jaw hair, and manes are incised or striated. Between relief borders the field is decorated with incised C-shaped spirals and double lines. The central part of the inner edge has a bow-shaped extension, carved partly in relief and partly in the round. Two perforations appear, one below the apex, and one below the ears of one of the tigers. The circular terminals of the slit mouths could also serve as suspension holes. The jade is an even yellowish-gray in color.

41 Plaque with Human Torso. Warring States.
5th–3rd century B.C.
Jade. H. 1⅛ in. B60J766.

The design of this rectangular plaque with identical sides, oval section, and vertical perforation is largely carved in openwork. The facial features of the large, semi-circular one-eared head are cursorily incised. A wide-lapeled garment adorned with incised chevrons and spirals covers the triangular bust. Distorted and disarticulated arms, bending at right angles at the elbows, complete the rectangular frame. Both arms are striated lengthwise. The even, ivory tint is due to calcification.

Published: Salmony, *Chinese Jade*, Pl. XXI:2.

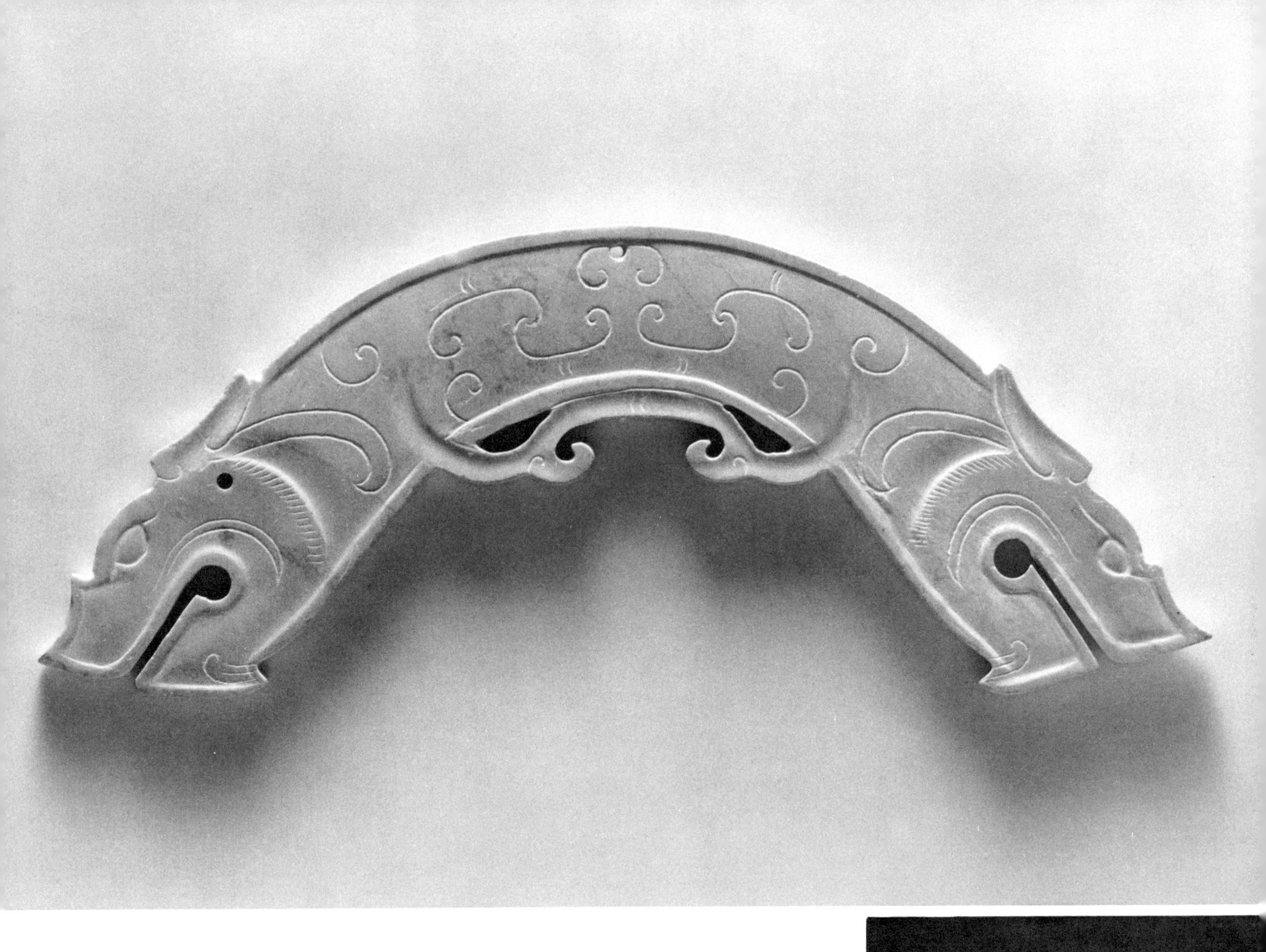

42 Bull's Head Pendant. Warring States.
5th–3rd century B.C.
Jade. H. 1 in. B60J765.

Large, flat, pointed horns with three deep vertical incisions surmount this bull's head, which is fully modeled in the round. The large eyes are in relief, the ears free-sculptured, and the nostrils incised. A suspension hole appears in the center of the forehead. A lower jaw is indicated, but the reverse is flat. The jade is a translucent white, with tan markings in the areas of the horns and the tip of the right ear.

43 Recumbent Buffalo. Han.
206 B.C.–A.D. 220.
Jade. L. 7⅜ in. B60J18+.

The compact contours are derived from the original shape of a small boulder. The massive head has a squared-off muzzle, large, fluted ram-like horns whose curling tips rest on the cheeks, and fully modeled ears. The eyes are incised; the eyebrows are striated, as is a star-like tuft of hair on top of the skull. Nostrils and lips are indicated by fairly deep carving. The animal's body is bulky and without surface details except for the striated tail and pasterns. The hooves are carefully executed, not only all around but also underneath the body. The jade is grayish-green with brownish and black markings.

Published: Salmony, *Chinese Jade*, Pl. XXXVI; d'Argencé, *Apollo*, p. 135, Fig. 2(b).

Jades

45 **Pig.** Six Dynasties or Early T'ang. *(lower right)*
6th–7th century A.D.
Jade. L. 3⅝ in. B65J3.

The animal rests on its voluminous belly but its head is raised and alert. The rounded contours are barely disturbed by the sketchy surface details which indicate ears, limbs, and tail. The eyes are carved in relief, the nostrils are perforated. The weathered brown jade has many "worm marks."

Published: d'Argencé, *Apollo*, p. 136, Fig. 3(a).

44 **Squatting Monster.** Six Dynasties. *(upper left)*
4th–6th century A.D.
Jade. H. 2¼ in. B65J34.

The monster sits with its rear paws joined in front of its bulging abdomen. It has the body of a bear, the head of a batrachian, and two long, curving horns which rest on its shoulders. Nail marks suggest breasts and navel. All four paws are striated, as is the long pointed beard. The bulging eyes are done in relief, and mouth and chin are indicated by two long incisions. The right forepaw holds a rattle, the left prayer beads. It may be that the monster is a caricature of a monk. The color is grayish-green with black markings.

46 **Camel.** T'ang. *(upper right)*
618–907 A.D.
Jade. L. 3¼ in. B60J869.

All four legs are folded underneath this reclining camel. The head is twisted backward and the mouth bites the forehump. The animal is treated realistically, but no surface details are shown except for striations to describe hair on the neck and humps, and incisions for the eyes. The undersides of the feet, however, are fully modeled. The jade is tan with brown markings.

Published: d'Argencé, *Apollo*, p. 136, Fig. 3(c).

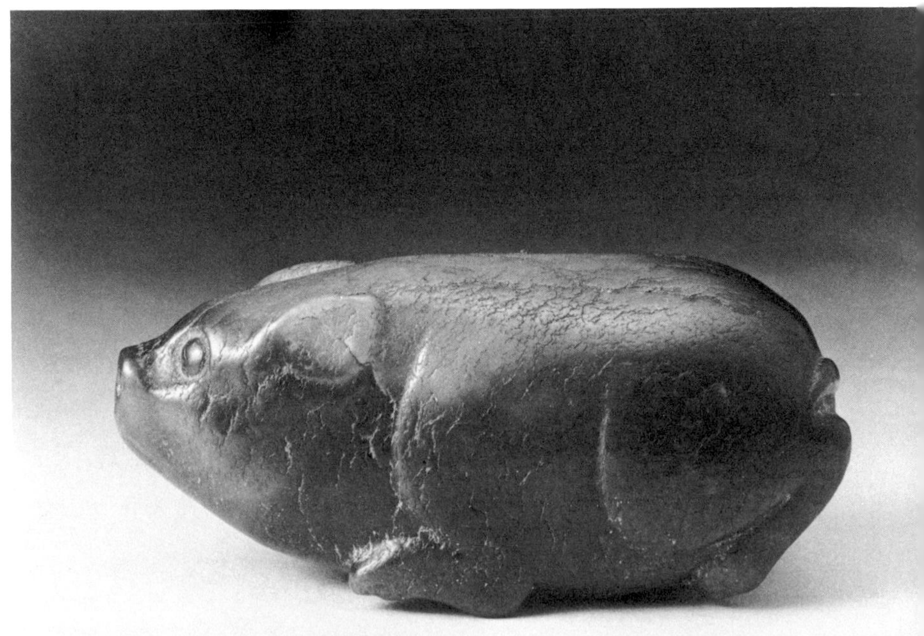

Jades

47 **Bird Ornament.** T'ang.
618–907 A.D.
Jade. H. 3¼ in. B65J15.

The bird's body is elongated, and arched to the point where one of the tail feathers rests on the flattened crest. Facial features and wing feathers are incised in a fairly realistic manner, and the movement of the large, curving tail feathers is emphasized by purely calligraphic lines. The legs, tucked up against the body, are rendered in relief. The underside is perforated and the object probably served as a head ornament. The color is light green with brown markings.

48 **Buffalo.** Ming.
1368–1644 A.D.
Jade. L. 8⅜ in. B60J17+.

This buffalo rests in the same position as that of No. 43, but here the head is freely sculptured. The treatment is realistic, even though surface details are reduced to a minimum—fluting for the flat horns, incisions for eyes, nostrils, and mouth, and striations for hair on tail and ears. The legs and dewlap are rendered in high relief but the undersides of legs and hooves are treated cursorily. The jade is light green with brown markings.

Published: d'Argencé, *Asia Foundation*, Fig. 16.

Jades

49 **Mountain.** Ch'ing.
17th–18th century A.D.
Jade. H. 6¾ in., W. 9 in. B60J26.

A boulder carved in high relief shows Buddhist scenes in landscape settings. On one side of the boulder is shown P'u-hsien, the Bodhisattva of benevolence, paying a visit to Wen-shu, the Bodhisattva of wisdom. P'u-hsien, mounted on his white elephant, holding a sceptre and followed by an attendant with the sacred umbrella, is at the bottom of a flight of steps presumably leading to his heavenly retreat. Wen-shu sits in meditation in a cave surrounded by an architectural balustrade. A youthful attendant holds in leash his usual vehicle, the Lion. The whole scene is permeated by a slightly humoristic touch. On the other side is carved a mountain landscape with a three-story pagoda. The color is a translucent, light green with brown markings.

Published: d'Argencé, *Asia Foundation,* Fig. 17.

50 **Brush-holder.** Ch'ing.
18th century A.D.
Jade. H. 7 in., Diam. 8⅛ in. B60J29.

The entire surface of this thick-walled cylinder is decorated with a scene inspired, probably, by a contemporary landscape painting. Pilgrims, hunters, and a procession of horsemen carrying banners and ritual objects ride along mountainous paths. Lakes and peaks can be seen in the background, rocks, trees, and waves in the foreground. Cloud-shaped scrolls appear under the rim of the brush-holder. The vessel, which rests on five short feet, is of spinach-green jade with brown specks.

Published: d'Argencé, *Apollo*, p. 137, Pl. XV.

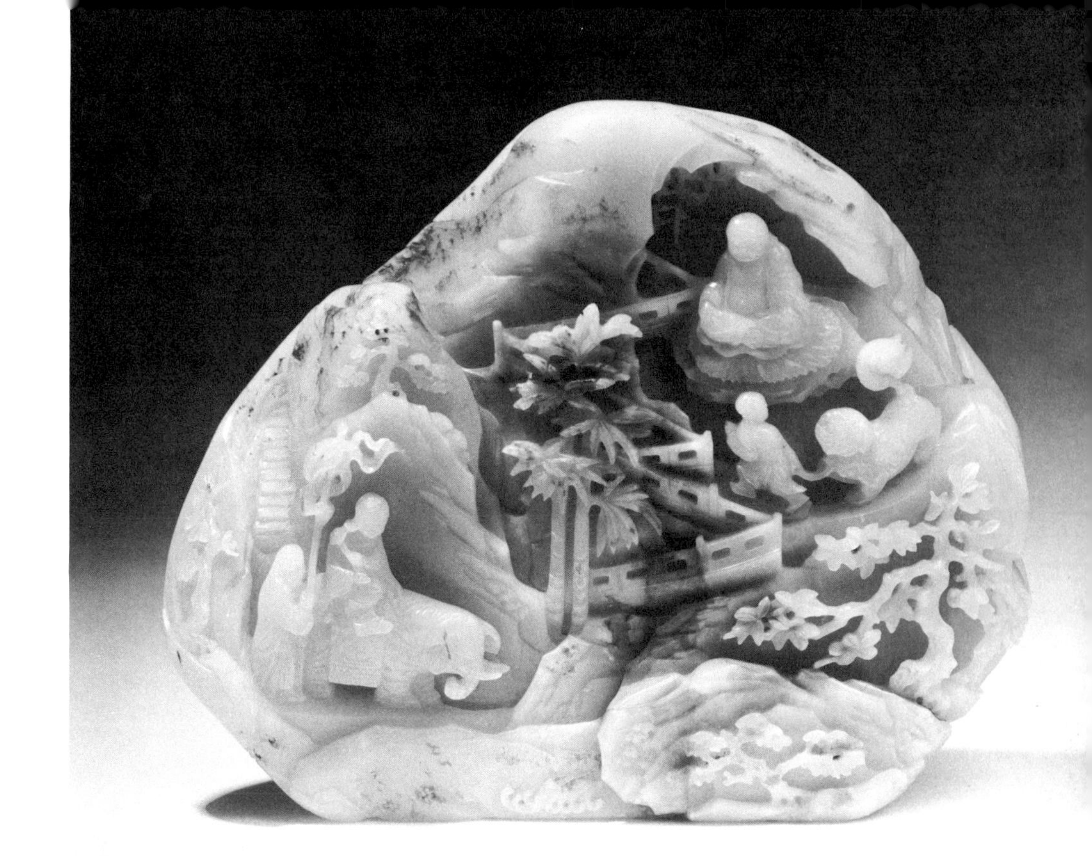

Jades

51 **Hu-shaped Vase.** Ch'ing.
Ch'ien Lung period, dated 1789.
Jade. H. 18 in., W. 9½ in. B60J36.

This thick-walled vessel is carved in the shape of a bronze *Hu* with large, vertical lug handles and a stepped foot. Both sides are identical. Most of the ornamental schemes, such as meanders on the lip, hanging blades on the neck, and a composite *t'ao-t'ieh* mask on the belly, are derived from those of archaic bronze vessels (see for instance No. 15). On the other hand, the borders framing the central zone are borrowed from prototypes developed by Ming and Early Ch'ing ceramists. A long inscription is incised on the lower part of the neck and filled in with gold paint. The color is dark green.

Published: S. H. Hansford, *Exhibition of Chinese Jades*, The Oriental Ceramic Society, London, 1948, Pl. X: No. 163.

Lapis Lazuli

52 **Mountain.** Ch'ing.
Ch'ien Lung period. 1736–1795 A.D.
Lapis lazuli. H. 9¼ in., W. 13 in. B60J31.

A Taoist scene in a landscape setting is carved in high relief on this boulder. On a rocky mountain, an immortal and his attendant collect the fungus of immortality. Above are the roofs of a temple, below, a torrent; a crane, symbol of longevity, flies high above. On the reverse appears another mountain scene with deer and pine trees, also symbols of longevity. On one of the flat rocks is a forty-nine character inscription, incised and filled with gold paint. According to this inscription, which reproduces a text written by Ch'ien Lung himself, the scene was inspired by a painting by Ch'iu Ying, the famous early sixteenth century artist. The color is bright blue with off-white markings.

Ceramics

53 **Urn.** Neolithic. Yang-Shao culture.
Ma-ch'ang type. Ca. 2000–1500 B.C.
Pottery. H. 14¼ in., Diam. 14 in. B60P1110.

This tall, globular urn is of reddish-buff pottery ornamented with anthropomorphic shapes and large medallions on the upper part of the body. Chevrons appear on the neck, and short parallel lines inside the lip. The various motifs are painted in black and red. The urn has a cylindrical neck, everted mouth rim, two loop handles, and a flat base.

Published: d'Argencé, *Apollo*, p. 85, Pl. I; d'Argencé, *A.B.C. Ceramics*, Pl. III.

Ceramics

54 **Stem-Cup.** Late Shang. *(upper left)*
An-yang type. 1300–1028 B.C.
White Pottery. H. 6 in., Diam. 9½ in. B60P527.

T'ao-t'ieh masks and meanders are carved on the cup and in two narrow belts on the stem of this vessel. The central zone of the stem shows three rows of whorl circles. It has a wide, flaring foot and thick, beveled mouth rim. The item is partly reconstructed.

Published: S. Umehara, *Kanan Anyō-Ibutsu no Kenkyū*, Kyoto, 1941, Pl. II; d'Argencé, *Apollo*, p. 89, Fig. 10.

55 **Yi.** Warring States. *(lower right)*
Yüeh type. 5th–3rd century B.C.
Stoneware. H. 6 in., Diam. 4 in. B60P225.

This tripod in the shape of a bronze *Yi* has a basin-like body with a triangular projection surmounted by a monster's head with crenellated horns. The vessel rests on short, baluster legs and has sturdy S-shaped handles. The material is buff stoneware, glazed and decorated with a close-knit ornament of stamped spirals.

Published: W. Hochstadter, *BMFEA*, No. 24 (1952), Pl. 27, Fig. 106; La Plante, *Arts of the Chou Dynasty*, No. 321; d'Argencé, *Apollo*, p. 90, Fig. 14; d'Argencé, *A.B.C. Ceramics*, Pl. VIII:A.

56 **Hu.** Late Warring States or Western Han.
3rd–1st century B.C. *(upper left)*
Pottery. H. 23 in., Diam. 16 in. B60P2391.

This *Hu* has a globular body set on a high ring foot. The dome-shaped lid has slots for the insertion of three S-shaped knobs (now missing). Two *t'ao-t'ieh* masks in relief, with loops, are set on the shoulders. The vessel is of dark gray pottery, with scrolls and interlocked "birdicized clouds" painted in red, white, and indigo with red outlines.

Published: La Plante, *Arts of the Chou Dynasty*, No. 207; d'Argencé, *Apollo*, p. 91, Fig. 17; d'Argencé, *A.B.C. Ceramics*, Pl. IX:B.

57 **Po-shan-lu.** Han. *(lower right)*
206 B.C.–A.D. 221.
Pottery. H. 9 in., Diam. 7¼ in. B60P203.

The high, conical lid of this incense burner bears a carved design of hunters, dogs, game, and various kinds of quadrupeds, birds, and reptiles set against a background of hills and trees. The object is made of buff, unglazed pottery in the shape of a stem-cup rising from a basin-like foot. The lid has many triangular perforations.

Published: d'Argencé, *A.B.C. Ceramics* Pl. X:B.

58 **Dog.** Han.
Ch'ang-sha type. 206 B.C.–A.D. 221.
Pottery. H. 14¾ in., L. 13½ in. B60P83+.

This seated watchdog barks as his tail wags. His large head tops a long, pillar-like neck; his face is square, with a flat forehead and eyes in relief; the moustache is incised. The dog's ears are leaf-like and the legs stumpy. A thick, brown glaze covers the red pottery.

Published: Sickman, *Selections from the Avery Brundage Collection*, No. 44; d'Argencé, *Apollo*, p. 92, Fig. 19; d'Argencé, *A.B.C. Ceramics*, Pl. XI:A.

59 **Farmyard.** Han.
206 B.C.–A.D. 221.
Pottery. H. 4 in., L. 8¾ in. B60P229.

In a corner of a walled yard, a farmer pounds grain; next to him is a large millstone. A dog and two domestic fowl watch the scene. The pottery is gray with an iridescent green glaze.

Published: d'Argencé, *A.B.C. Ceramics*, Pl. XII:B.

Ceramics

60 **Bowl.** Wu or Western Chin. *(below)*
Yüeh type. 3rd–4th century A D.
Stoneware. H. 1⅞ in., Diam. 4 in. B60P1757.

A pillar rising from the center of the deep bowl supports two small, kissing birds with extended wings and turned-up tails. Their feathers are indicated by simple comb marks. The mouth and foot rim of the bowl are irregular. The base is concave, glazed, and shows five gritty kiln marks. The gray stoneware has a transparent grayish-green glaze.

Published: d'Argencé, *Apollo*, p. 94, Fig. 23.

61 **Covered Bowl.** Six Dynasties. *(above)*
Yüeh type. 4th–5th century A.D.
Stoneware. H. 3 in., Diam. 4 in. B60P145.

A dome-shaped lid with a bud-like knob covers this wide, globular bowl set on a shallow ring foot. The gray stoneware bears a transparent, yellowish-green glaze enhanced by a symmetrical arrangement of iron-brown spots. The base is unglazed and shows five gritty kiln marks.

Published: d'Argencé, *Apollo*, p. 94, Fig. 24; d'Argencé, *A.B.C. Ceramics*, Pl. XIV:D.

Ceramics

62 Young Lady with Hand Warmer. Early T'ang.
7th–8th century A.D.
Pottery. H. 10 in. B60P299.

A young lady, a tomb figurine, wears a collarless, high-waisted, pleated dress with long sleeves. Her hair is arranged in plaits high on her head. In her arms she carries a hand warmer similar to No. 63. The hollow, gray pottery is covered by a thin, creamy glaze which stops short of the base.

63 Hand Warmer. Early T'ang.
7th–8th century A.D.
Pottery. H. 8 in., W. 8 in. B60P140.

This beehive-shaped hand warmer rests on a flat base and has a circular opening at the top. Lattice-like apertures and rosettes ornament the shoulder. It is of buff pottery with a white, creamy glaze over a white slip. The base is unglazed.

Ceramics

64 **Horse.** T'ang.
680–750 A.D.
Pottery. H. 14⅜ in., L. 18 in. B60P22+.

The horse, in full harness with high saddle and stirrups, stands on a rectangular, unglazed base. His head, which is small in proportion to his body, is turned sideways; his mane and tail are docked. The straps and harness are decorated with tassels in high relief; the unglazed saddle is painted in ochre with a floral pattern in red, white, and aubergine. A three-color glaze with streaks of blue, amber, and brown on a creamy ground covers the animal, a hollow tomb figurine in hard-fired pottery.

Published: d'Argencé, *Apollo*, p. 97, Pl. V; d'Argencé, *A.B.C. Ceramics*, Pl. XXV:A.

65 **Tray.** T'ang. *(lower right)*
680–750 A.D.
Pottery. H. 2⅛ in., Diam. 11 in. B60P524.

The tray is six-lobed and stands on three short feet. It is of buff-white pottery with crystal-shaped motifs in brown, blue, and green on a yellow ground. The central part of the base and the feet are unglazed, but the periphery is covered by a deep, rich, brown glaze.

Published: d'Argencé, *Apollo*, p. 96, Fig. 30; d'Argencé, *A.B.C. Ceramics*, Pl. XXVI:A.

66 **Small Plate.** T'ang. *(upper left)*
Hsing-yao type. 8th–9th century A.D.
Porcelain. Diam. 5⅜ in. B60P1392.

On the bottom of this plate with an irregular foliated rim is an impressed and combed design suggestive of an open lotus flower. The unglazed base is slightly concave. The porcelain is a light gray body with a transparent glaze over a white slip.

Published: d'Argencé, *A.B.C. Ceramics*, Pl. XX:C.

Ceramics

67 **Ewer.** T'ang. *(lower right)*
Southern type. 7th–8th century A.D.
Stoneware. H. 7⅛ in. B60P1807.

The beehive-shaped body, with narrow neck, everted mouth rim, and three-stranded handle, is set on a flat base with a reinforced foot rim. Three molded leaf motifs appear below the short, hexagonal spout and the small, lateral, three-stranded loops. It is of buff stoneware with an olive green glaze stopping short of the base. The leaf motifs are covered by a thick layer of brown glaze. The base is unglazed.

Published: d'Argencé, *A.B.C. Ceramics*, Pl. XIX:A.

68 **Ewer.** Five Dynasties or Early Sung. *(upper left)*
Yüeh type. 10th century A.D.
Stoneware. H. 6½ in. B60P2380.

This ewer has a cup-shaped mouth, a tall, slender neck with three grooves near the base, a six-paneled pear-shaped body, and a shallow spreading foot. Two small loops are placed on the stepped shoulder. The spout and handle are large and casually modelled. It is of gray porcelaneous stoneware with an over-all grayish-green glaze. Four gritty kiln marks remain on the base.

Published: d'Argencé, *Apollo*, p. 102, Fig. 37; d'Argencé, *A.B.C. Ceramics*, Pl. XXIX:B.

69 **Cup-stand.** Sung.
Northern Celadon. 11th–12th century A.D.
Porcelain. H. 7 in., Diam. 7 in. B60P1379.

The deep, reel-like, reticulated body has a large, dome-shaped lip decorated with a carved peony scroll. The ringed stem rises from a high, reticulated foot in the shape of an inverted cup. It is of porcelaneous stoneware with an olive green glaze.

Published: Garner, *Apollo*, p. 128, Fig. 1; d'Argencé, *A.B.C. Ceramics*, Pl. XXX:B.

70 **Plate.** Sung.
Ting ware. 10th–12th century A.D.
Porcelain. Diam. 10¼ in. B60P82+.

An incised design of flowering plants is carved on the inside and an incised, leafy scroll pattern appears on the rim of this shallow plate. The flat, everted rim is fitted with a copper band. There is a shallow foot, and the base is slightly concave. The porcelain is covered by a creamy, white glaze inside and out.

Published: Sickman, *Selections from the Avery Brundage Collection,* No. 53.

71 **Pillow.** Sung. *(above)*
Tz'u-chou ware. 10th–13th century A.D.
Stoneware. W. 11⅝ in. B65P51.

The top of this leaf-shaped, or fungus-shaped, head-rest is decorated with a deer surrounded by cloud-shaped fungi—symbols of longevity. Hollow and concave, it rests on a semicircular support. The stoneware was covered first with white slip, then black; the designs were obtained by scraping away a portion of the black layer to reveal the white ground, retaining the motifs in black. There is a transparent, neutral overglaze.

Published: d'Argencé, *A.B.C. Ceramics*, Pl. XL:A.

73 **Tea Bowl.** Sung. *(below)*
Chien ware. 10th–13th century A.D.
Stoneware. H. 2¾ in., Diam. 7¾ in. B60P1718.

This deep, conical bowl, with thick everted lip and small shallow foot, is covered by a thick, black glaze which stops short of the foot. Dense, star-like, silvery spots appear over the entire inside surface.

Published: d'Argencé, *A.B.C. Ceramics*, Pl. XLVI:B.

72 **Mei P'ing Vase.** Late Sung or Yüan.
Chün ware. 13th–14th century A.D.
Stoneware. H. 4 in. B60P19+.

Tall, slender, with an ovoid body, short constricted neck, and thick, projecting mouth rim, this vase is of gray stoneware—turned brown when exposed to fire. A thick, turquoise-blue glaze bearing purple splashes and brown spots stops short of the base. The glaze is pitted with characteristic "pin-holes."

Published: Garner, *Apollo*, p. 127, Pl. XIII; d'Argencé, *A.B.C. Ceramics*, Pl. XXXV.

74 **Altar Jar.** Late Northern Sung.
Lung-ch'üan ware. Ca. 11th century A.D.
Porcelain. H. 9½ in., Diam. 5 in. B62P147.

The jar has an ovoid body on a short circular foot. The lip of the dome-shaped lid overhangs the flaring mouth. A sculptured dragon encircles the neck, and a small reclining dog rests on the lid. A molded band of petals surrounds the lower part of the body. The porcelain is covered by a rich smooth celadon glaze; the base is unglazed.

Published: d'Argencé, *A.B.C. Ceramics*, Pl. XLIII.

Ceramics

75 **Bowl.** Late Southern Sung or Yüan.
Kuan ware. 13th–14th century A.D.
Porcelain. Diam. 4⅝ in. B62P149.

This deep bowl with flaring sides, six-foil lip, and shallow foot is of blackish-brown stoneware with boldly crackled glaze inside and out.

Published: d'Argencé, *A.B.C. Ceramics*, Pl. XLV:C.

76 **Incense Burner.** Sung.
Ch'ing-pai ware. 10th–13th century A.D.
Porcelain. H. 5¼ in. B60P1764.

The lid, the upper part of which is reticulated, and the bowl form a sphere. The sphere rests on a short, ringed stem which rises from a hollow, fluted, splayed foot with a scalloped rim. The porcelain has a high, transparent, pale blue glaze.

Published: *Catalogue of the International Exhibition of Chinese Art at the Royal Academy of Arts*, London, 1935, p. 936, Fig. 940; Garner, *Apollo*, p. 131, Fig. 4; d'Argencé, *A.B.C. Ceramics*, Pl. XLI.

Ceramics

77 **Jar.** Yüan. *(upper left)*
Ch'ing-pai ware. Early 14th century A.D.
Porcelain. H. 12½ in., Diam. 13 in. B60P48.

This jar has a globular body with high shoulders, a short straight neck, and a reinforced mouth rim. The shoulder bears a floral design. Dragons and waves are seen on the belly, framed between horizontal grooves, and a band of conventionalized lotus petals appears on the lower part of the body. All of these patterns are combed or freely incised. The porcelain is covered with thin pale blue glaze; the base is unglazed.

Published: d'Argencé, *A.B.C. Ceramics*, Pl. XLVIII:A.

78 **Vase and Stand.** Yüan. *(lower right)*
Ch'ing-pai ware. 14th century A.D.
Porcelain. H. 9½ in., Diam. 4½ in. B60P22.

The inverted pear-shaped body of the base is decorated with molded lotus sprays and cranes, alternating with gadroons. It has a high, conical neck and a tall, slender foot which rests on the bottom of the stand. The latter is supported by three small feet and has six large keyhole-shaped openings on the side. These openings are outlined with pearl-bead decoration, a device also used for the bowstrings and the gadroons on the body of the vase. The porcelain is covered with a pale bluish glaze.

Published: Garner, *Apollo*, p. 131, Fig. 7; d'Argencé, *A.B.C. Ceramics*, Pl. XLVIII:B.

Ceramics

79 **Stem-cup.** Yüan. *(upper left)*
First half 14th century A.D.
Porcelain. H. 3⅝ in., Diam. 4⅜ in. B65P54.

This cup-shaped container with everted mouth rim stands on a high, hollow, conical, ringed support. Underglaze designs are painted in blue on the porcelain. On the outside of the cup is a dragon chasing a flaming pearl. On the bottom of the interior is a floral spray, and on the inside of the rim a border of scrolled tendrils. The base and the inside of the foot are unglazed.

Published: d'Argencé, *A.B.C. Ceramics*, Pl. XLIX:B.

80 **Stem-cup.** Ming. *(lower right)*
Hsüan Te period. 1426–1435 A.D.
Porcelain. H. 4 in., Diam. 4 in. B60P1512.

The lid is missing from this globular container with a short stem and flaring foot. Underglaze designs, a zigzag and triangle border on the neck and a wide floral band on the belly, are painted in blue on the porcelain; rows of petals embrace the base of the bowl and the upper part of the foot.

Published: d'Argencé, *A.B.C. Ceramics*, Pl. L:B.

81 **Bowl.** Ming. *(lower left)*
Hsüan Te period. 1426–1435 A.D.
Porcelain. H. 2⅞ in., Diam. 6 in. B60P2354.

A blue wreath of flowers between two narrow bands of floral and geometrical patterns is painted underglaze on this small porcelain bowl. It has a depressed globular shape and a thick, slightly flaring mouth. There is a thin blue line inside the mouth rim. A six-character Hsüan Te mark appears high on the shoulder.

Published: d'Argencé, *A.B.C. Ceramics*, Pl. L:C.

82 **Jar.** Early Ming. *(upper right)*
Early 15th century A.D.
Porcelain. H. 8½ in., Diam. 10 in. B60P245.

Underglaze designs are painted in blue on this large, globular, porcelain jar. There are bowstrings on the neck, variants of cloud-collar and formal floral patterns on the shoulder, a wide lotus scroll band on the belly, and floral sprays around the foot. The neck of the jar is short and straight, and the mouth rim reinforced. The small base is unglazed.

Published: Garner, *Apollo*, p. 131, Fig. 6; d'Argencé, *A.B.C. Ceramics*, Pl. LII:B.

大明宣德年製

大明宣德年製

83 **Bowl.** Ming.
Hung Chih period. 1488–1505 A.D.
Porcelain. H. 3½ in., Diam. 7⅛ in. B60P2079.

Dragons, left in reserve on the biscuit, decorate the outside and the bottom of this graceful bowl. A few details such as hair at the articulations and claws are incised under the glaze. The bowl has a rounded side and a slightly spreading lip. A six-character Hung Chih inscription appears on the base.

Published: d'Argencé, *A.B.C. Ceramics*, Pl. LVIII:A.

84 **Vase.** Early Ming.
Fa-hua type. First part of 16th century A.D.
Stoneware. H. 10 in., Diam. 5¼ in. B60P1608.

This bottle-shaped vase is of buff-white porcelaneous stoneware with a purple glaze stopping short of the base. The peony spray design is done in cloisonné technique. The outlines are made of fillets of applied clay, filled in with blue and white glazes.

CARL A. RUDISILL LIBRARY
LENOIR RHYNE COLLEGE

85 Fish Jar. Ming.
Chia Ching period. 1522–1566 A.D.
Porcelain. H. 17 in., Diam. 17 in. B60P78+.

Underglaze blue and variegated enamels of the "five-color" type decorate this globular, white porcelain jar. Fish swim amid lotus and other aquatic plants on the belly and on the dome-shaped cover with its bud-like knob. False gadroons appear on the shoulder and a petal border decorates the foot. There is a six-character Chia Ching mark in underglaze blue on the base.

Published: Garner, *Apollo*, p. 130, Pl. XIV.

86 **Vase.** Late Ming.
Wan Li period. 1573–1615 A.D.
Porcelain. H. 17 in., Diam. 9 in. B60P56.

This shape is a variant of the double-gourd, with pear-shaped body, elongated neck, bulbous mouth and short vertical rim. The white porcelain is decorated in underglaze blue and enamels of the "five-color" type. The motifs include: a cloud-scroll border on the rim; a floral scroll on the bulb; isolated floral sprays on the neck; zigzag and stylized flowers on the shoulder. On the belly there is a large band of dragons chasing flaming pearls amid realistic flowers. A key-fret border decorates the foot. A six-character Wan Li inscription in underglaze blue appears on the mouth rim.

Published: S. Jenyns, *Ming Pottery and Porcelain,* Faber and Faber, London, 1953, Pl. 100A.

Ceramics

87 Standing Figure. Late Ming or Early Ch'ing.
Te-hua ware. 17th century A.D.
Porcelain. H. 16½ in. B60P20+.

A scholar holds a scroll in his left hand. The pedestal of rocks and waves and the movement of the headdress and garment suggest a windy and rocky shore. The glassy-white porcelain is of the Blanc de Chine type. The delicate moustache is black.

Published: Garner, *Apollo*, p. 133, Fig. 12.

88 Vase. Ch'ing.
Famille Noire type. K'ang Hsi period. 1662–1722 A.D.
Porcelain. H. 5½ in. B60P1442.

This chalice-like vessel follows the shape of a bronze *Ku*, with flaring trumpet, long stem with bulbous central part, and spreading foot. The white porcelain is decorated in Famille Noire enamels. Various Buddhist and Taoist symbols are seen on the mouth and the upper part of the stem. Square meanders decorate the bulb, leaf borders the upper and lower parts of the stem.

89 **Vase.** Ch'ing. *(upper left)*
K'ang Hsi period. 1662–1722 A.D.
Porcelain. H. 6¼ in. B60P1312.

This bottle-shaped vase has a squat, globular body and a long, wide neck, spreading slightly at the mouth. The white porcelain is covered with a boldly crackled apple-green glaze; the base is unglazed.

Published: d'Argencé, *A.B.C. Ceramics*, Pl. LXV:B.

90 **Vase.** Ch'ing. *(lower left)*
Yung Cheng period. 1723–1735 A.D.
Porcelain. H. 10 in. B60P16.

Rings circle the neck, shoulder, body, and foot of this Mei-p'ing shape with a short neck. The white porcelain is covered with a tea-dust glaze. A four-seal-character Yung Cheng inscription is incised on the base.

Published: d'Argencé, *A.B.C. Ceramics*, Pl. LXX:C.

91 **Ewer.** Ch'ing. *(lower right)*
Yung Cheng period. 1723–1735 A.D.
Porcelain. H. 10 in. B60P13.

Rows of petals are modeled on the shoulder and above the foot of this cylindrical ewer. Floral patterns are incised on the shoulder, the central field, and the long, ringed neck, which ends in a spouted mouth. It is of white porcelain with a celadon glaze. A six-seal-character Yung Cheng inscription appears in underglaze blue on the base.

Published: Garner, *Apollo*, p. 132, Fig. 11; d'Argencé, *A.B.C. Ceramics*, Pl. LXX:B.

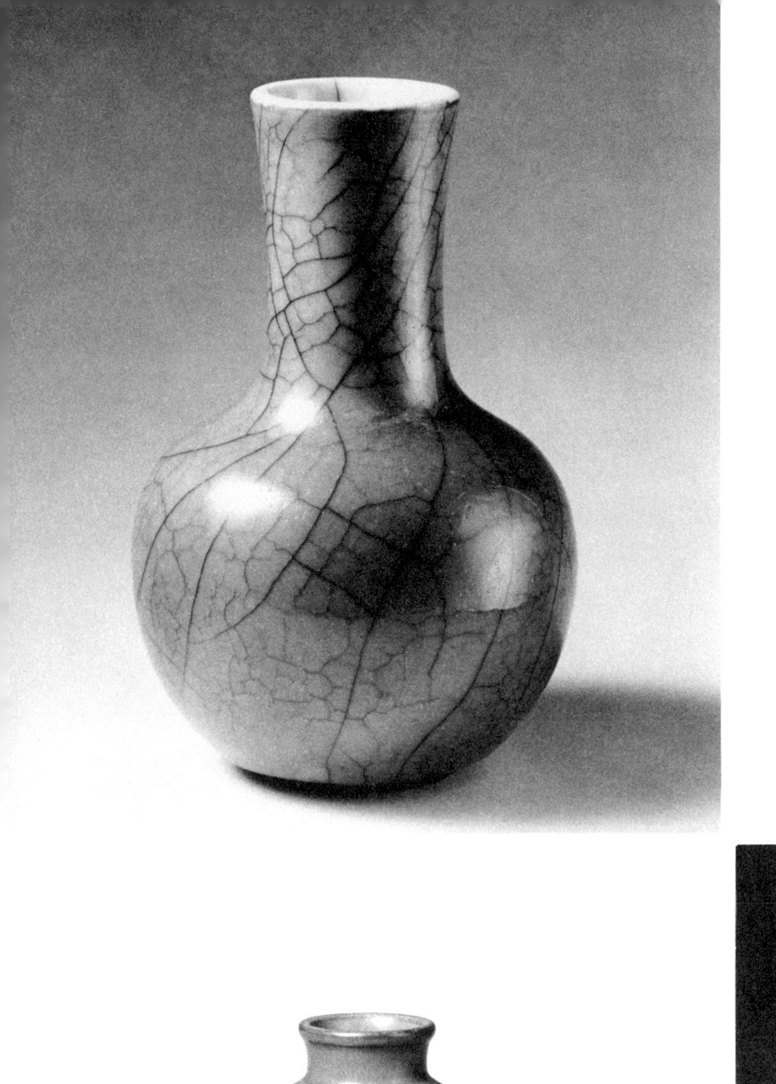

92 Small Plate. Ch'ing.
Famille Rose type. Yung Cheng period. 1723–1735 A.D.
Porcelain. Diam. 5¼ in. B60P1697.

This white porcelain plate is decorated in Famille Rose enamels with a pair of quail sheltering on a rocky bank amid a variety of plants and flowers, including narcissi and fungi. A six-character Yung Cheng inscription in underglaze blue appears on the base.

Published: d'Argencé, *A.B.C. Ceramics*, Pl. LXXIII:A.

93 Pair of Bowls. Ch'ing.
Mille Fleurs type. Chia Ch'ing period. 1796–1821 A.D.
Porcelain. Diam. 5⅛ in. B60P2095, B60P2096.

Flowers in engraved lines and Famille Rose enamels cover these deep bowls. In each the foot is straight, the lip slightly spreading. Each bears a six-seal-character Chia Ch'ing inscription in underglaze blue on the base, and the rest of the base is covered with a turquoise blue glaze.

Published: d'Argencé, *A.B.C. Ceramics*, Pl. LXXIV:B.

94 Yü-shang Cup. Warring States or Early Western Han. *(above)*
Ch'ang-sha style. 5th–2nd century B.C.
Lacquered wood. L. 6⅞ in. B66M3.

Geometric designs in red on a black ground are painted on this deep, oval cup with semi-circular lateral ears. On the inner side of the walls the ornamental scheme is interrupted by two horizontal bands in plain red.

95 Yü-shang Cup. Warring States or Early Western Han. *(below)*
Ch'ang-sha style. 5th–2nd century B.C.
Lacquered wood. L. 6⅜ in. B66M2.

This shallow, oval cup with lateral ears is decorated with geometric designs painted in red on a black ground. The bottom of the cup is solid red.

96 **Box.** Early Ming.
First half of 15th century A.D.
Lacquered wood. Diam. 4⅞ in. B65M16.

Various floral motifs are carved on the top and sides of this cylindrical box. Painted red, they stand in high relief against a buff ground. The lid fits over a high, thin, vertical mouth rim. The inside is plain brown. The base, also brown, bears a six-character Yung Lo inscription which was scratched through the lacquer, and may be a later addition.

97 **Kuan Ti.** Ming.
15th century A.D.
Ivory. H. 11 in. B60S299.

Kuan Ti, the God of War, is seated on a high chair resting on a flat, circular pedestal and covered by the skin of a tiger whose head serves as the God's foot-rest. Kuan Ti wears an official dress. His theatrical pose is typical of the classical Chinese opera.

Published: Garner, *Apollo*, p. 146, Fig. 8.

Decorative Arts

98 **Box.** Late Ming.
Early 17th century A.D.
Bamboo and lacquered wood. H. 4¾ in., L. 19 in., W. 13½ in. B60M427.

The sides of this rectangular box with rounded sides are made of woven bamboo panels set in wooden frames. A large panel on the lid shows an audience scene in the foreground and a mountainous landscape in the background. The scene is painted in brilliant colors, outlined in gold on a black ground. The wood frames and the six feet are decorated in gold paint with flowers and birds. The interior and the underside of the box are plain black.

Published: H. M. Garner, "A Group of Chinese Lacquers with Basketry Panels," *Archives of Asian Art*, No. XX, 1966–1967, pp. 6–24.

99 **Basin.** Ch'ing.
Ch'ien Lung period. 1736–1795 A.D.
Cloisonné. H. 10⅝ in., Diam. 24½ in. B60M10+.

The bronze walls and base of this vessel are decorated inside and out with multi-colored, copper-wired enamels. A bronze band with an incised meander pattern encircles the mouth rim. Inside, fish and other water animals swim among water plants on a turquoise blue ground. The outside illustrates the theme of "The Hundred Deer," in a landscape of mountains and trees against a cloudy background of white. The turquoise blue base is decorated with disconnected plum blossoms.

Published: d'Argencé, *Asia Foundation*, Pl. XIV.

Gilt Bronze Sculpture

100 Seated Buddha. Posterior Chao dynasty.
Dated 338 A.D. *(frontispiece)*
Gilt bronze. H. 15½ in., W. 9⅝ in. B60B1034.

This is the earliest dated piece of Chinese Buddhist sculpture known. The Buddha is seated in meditation on a rectangular pedestal. The back and neck are bent gently forward, and the palm of one hand is placed against the back of the other. The rounded face has high eyebrows, almond-shaped eyes, a short nose, and slightly smiling lips. On the back of the head is a tenon for the attachment of a halo, now missing. A long garment covering the body and legs falls in cascading folds. The frame of the pedestal is casually decorated with incised floral scrolls and the central plate is perforated with three holes for the attachment of appliqués, now missing. An inscription, partly damaged, is incised on the back of the pedestal. The sculpture is of gilt bronze, with incrustations. Both statuette and pedestal are hollow.

Published: C. T. Loo, *An Exhibition of Ancient Chinese Ritual Bronzes*, New York, 1941–1942, No. 92; A. F. Wright, *Buddhism in Chinese History*, Stanford, California, 1959, Pl. I; S. Mizuno, *Bronze and Stone Sculpture of China*, Tokyo, 1960, Pl. 88; B. Rowland, *The Evolution of the Buddha Image*, New York, 1963, Pl. 37; D. Seckel, *The Art of Buddhism*, New York, 1964, Pl. 23; W. Willetts, *Foundations of Chinese Art*, London, 1965, Pl. 119; Soper, *Apollo*, p. 104, Pl. IX; d'Argencé, *Asia Foundation*, Cover Plate.

101 Standing Bodhisattva. Northern Wei.
Mid-5th century A.D.
Gilt bronze. H. 5¾ in. B60B638.

The Bodhisattva stands on a lotus pedestal supported by a dais. Although treated frontally, the figurine suggests a slight walking movement which is emphasized by the arched posture of the body and the garment's rhythmical lines. The head, with long hair and tripartite crown, is relatively massive. The voluminous torso is bare except for a necklace and a shawl draped around shoulders and elbows, whence it falls freely along the legs. The waist and legs are covered by a thin dhoti. The concave back is equipped with two tenons for the attachment of a large nimbus, now missing.

Published: Soper, *Apollo*, p. 103, Fig. 1.

Gilt Bronze Sculpture

102 **Buddhist Shrine.** Northern Wei.
Dated 472 A.D.
Gilt bronze. H. 6¼ in. B60B1035.

Two small Buddhas are seated in meditation in front of a large, leaf-shaped nimbus and atop a high dais with splayed legs. The Buddhas have large heads with parted hair and chignon-like top-knots. They wear long, flowing garments that leave their right shoulders uncovered. The face of the nimbus is decorated in low relief with individual halos and flamed nimbi surmounted by a canopy with tassels. The rear is adorned by a large, seated Buddha, also in low relief. On the front legs of the dais are an incense burner, a box, and two donors in three-quarter view. The rear part bears the incised inscription. Floral and geometrical designs appear on the sides.

Gilt Bronze Sculpture

103 Altar Group. Early T'ang.
7th century A.D.
Gilt bronze. H. 12¾ in. B60B8+.

The central figure, Maitreya, is seated in Western manner on a high, rectangular throne rising from a dais whose upper part is decorated with incised lotus petals. The openwork nimbus is adorned with eight diminutive figurines of celestial beings, in the round. The dais rests on a large, rectangular platform with open, cusped sides, and is surrounded on three sides by nine free-standing figurines; two monks, two Bodhisattvas, two guardians, two lions, and a kneeling gnome carrying an incense burner on his head.

Published: H. Trubner, *The Arts of the T'ang Dynasty*, New York, 1961, Fig. 68.

Gilt Bronze Sculpture

104 **Kuvera** (?). T'ang. *(left)*
618–906 A.D.
Gilt bronze. H. 5 in. B60B512.

This gesticulating figure of a demon-like creature is seated on two small, nearly naked gnomes, seeming to crush them. The group is supported by a shallow, rock-shaped base. The main figure has an enormous head with almost bestial facial features; neck and arms are adorned with snakes. According to Professor Alexander Soper, "It is tempting to imagine that the group may have originated in the Gandhara formula that shows Kuvera as King of the Yaksas and god of wealth sitting with his consort Hariti in the midst of a brood of male children."

Published: Soper, *Apollo*, p. 106, Fig. 3.

105 **Kuan Yin.** T'ang. *(right)*
Late 7th–early 8th century A.D.
Gilt bronze. H. 13 in. B60B334.

Kuan Yin is standing in a graceful, swaying pose, with the right hip thrust out, on a lotus pedestal supported by a rectangular platform with open sides. The headdress is elaborate, with a small, seated Amitabha Buddha in front of the high top-knot. The bare torso is heavily adorned with flowing scarves and jewelry, the lower part of the body clad in a dhoti-type skirt which clings to the legs. In a nonchalant gesture, the raised right hand holds a willow spray, while the left hand holds a vase from which arises a lotus flower. There are five seated Buddhas in the periphery of the openwork nimbus. According to Professor A. Soper this aureole "is so much more broadly executed than the figure that it is probable that the two were assembled in modern times."

Published: Trubner, *Artibus Asiae*, Vol. XX 2/3 (1967), p. 105, Fig. 2; Trubner, *The Arts of the T'ang Dynasty*, Fig. 98; Soper, *Apollo*, p. 106, Fig. 4.

Gilt Bronze Sculpture

106 **Buddha Triad.** Probably Sung dynasty.
960–1279 A.D.
Gilt bronze. H. 8⅝ in., W. 7¼ in. B60B9+.

An embossed plaque shows a seated Buddha and two standing Bodhisattvas in high relief against plain, flattened nimbi. The Buddha sits cross-legged on a high, lotus pedestal supported by billowy scrolls simulating clouds or waves. The left hand rests on the left knee, the right hand is raised in a gesture of blessing or argumentation. The large head has half-closed eyes and a low, hemispherical *usnisa.* A long robe covering both shoulders and forming a series of concentric folds is derived from the Gandharan formula. The Bodhisattva on the right holds sprays of flowers in each hand; the one on the left holds a sword and a book. As explained by Professor A. Soper, this would indicate that they represent Kuan Yin and Wen Shu. Both attendants have bulky and slightly swaying bodies draped in the usual shawls and dhoti-like skirts bedecked with over-ornate jewelry. The crowned heads are turned slightly toward the Buddha.

Published: H. Munsterberg, *Artibus Asiae*, XI, 1/2 (1948), p. 38, Fig. 10; Trubner, *The Arts of the T'ang Dynasty*, No. 96: Soper, *Apollo*, p. 105, Fig. 2.

107 **Kuan Yin.** Yüan or Early Ming.
14th century A.D.
Gilt bronze. H. 13 in. B60S566.

Here Kuan Yin is seated in the position of ease *(lalitasana)*, the left leg pendant, the right knee raised and supporting the right arm. The large, rounded face has half-closed eyes. Plaited hair and a high, conical chignon adorn the head, which supports a small Amitabha Buddha in the round. An elaborate necklace with pendants covers most of the chest and the arms are bejeweled with two sets of bracelets.

108 **Stele.** Northern Ch'i.
From Ting-chou (Hopei).
Dated 551 A.D.
Marble. H. 22½ in. B60S279.

In the central position of this openwork stele, a Bodhisattva in princely attire is seated in meditation under two trees whose branches form a dome-shaped nimbus. Against a plain, circular halo, the Bodhisattva sits in Western fashion on a high throne, the right leg placed over the left knee. The left foot rests on a small lotus pedestal. The trunks of the trees are encircled by dragons; in the branches are six flying celestial beings and at the top a stupa. Two attendant Bodhisattvas stand on lotus pedestals next to the trunks. On the front of the rectangular base, in high relief, are a stupa, two lions, and two guardians in swaying posture. A fifty-one character dedicatory inscription is incised on the right side and on part of the back of the base. Many traces of original paint remain, including figures of donors on the right side and on the back of the base.

Stone Sculpture

109 **Pratyeka Buddha.** Northern Ch'i.
Probably from Hsiang-t'ang shan (Hopei).
Later part of 6th century A.D.
Limestone. H. 42 in. B60S153+.

The Buddha stands on a shallow, circular pedestal, the right leg slightly flexed, hands joined together in an attitude of prayer. The face is broad, with elongated, half-closed eyes, a thin nose, and a full, well-modeled mouth. The head-dress consists of plaited hair adorned with three curls and a conical *usnisa*. The long garment leaves the right side of the torso uncovered.

Published: Soper, *Apollo*, p. 106, Fig. 5.

Stone Sculpture

110 Headless Seated Buddha. Northern Ch'i or Sui.
Possibly from Ting-chou (Hopei).
Late 6th–early 7th century A.D.
Marble. H. 11 in. B60S9.

The head and hands of the Buddha are missing. The figure is seated on crossed legs, with the left leg on top. Three layers of garments are seen: a vest in direct contact with the skin; a shawl covering the shoulders and arms; and a robe crossing at the waist and covering the lower part of the body. One end of the robe rests on the left elbow. A quiet, but forceful rhythm animates these garments. Folds are suggested by broad, smooth planes delineated by deep incisions. The hem of the robe, below the feet, is rendered in a slightly more nervous manner.

Published: Soper, *Apollo*, p. 107, Fig. 6.

111 Bodhisattva. Mid T'ang.
From T'ien-lung shan (Shansi).
8th century A.D.
Sandstone. H. 28 in. B65S5.

The Bodhisattva, standing in an attitude of prayer, has a rounded face with youthful features. Plaited hair, a crown adorned with flowers, and a high top-knot, now partly missing, form the elaborate headdress. The torso is exposed and the shoulders are only partly covered by a shawl with flowing ends. The lower body is clad in a dhoti-type skirt.

Published: Sekino, *Tenryūzan Seki-butsushū*, Tokyo, 1928, Pl. 41 (head only); d'Argencé, *Asia Foundation*, Fig. 7.

Stone Sculpture

112 **Lohan.** Chin.
Dated 1180 A.D.
Marble. H. 42 in. B60S208.

The figure, dressed in monk's garments, stands on a lotus pedestal with the right leg brought forward; the right hand holds prayer beads, the left is raised with the palm outward. The head, slightly turned to the right, is rendered realistically with large deep-set eyes whose pupils are painted black, high cheek-bones, a wrinkled forehead, and curled eyebrows, moustache, and beard. The muscular neck and part of the bony chest are bare. A twenty-one character inscription is engraved on the front of the square base.

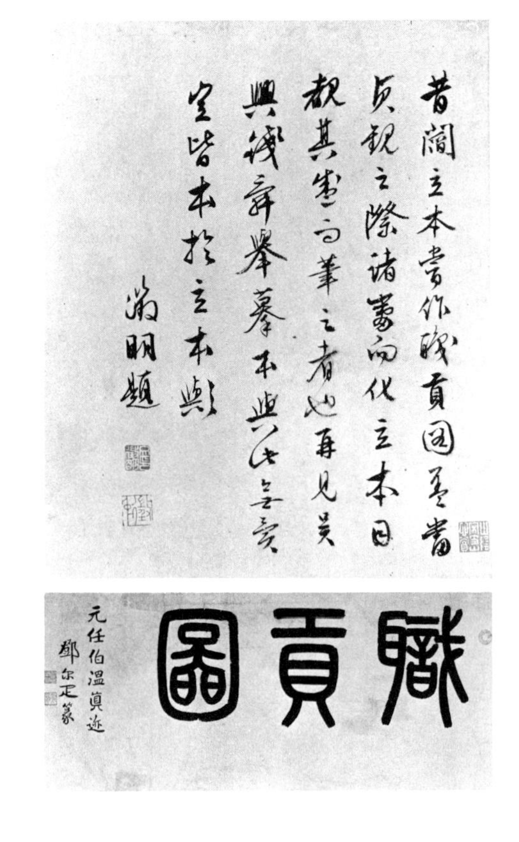

113 Tribute Bearers. Yüan.
Jen Po-wen. 14th century A.D.
Handscroll. Ink, gold, and colors on silk. L. 86¾ in., W. 14¼ in. B60D100.

This is a fragment of a longer scroll which illustrates the arrival of an embassy, probably from Central Asia. Six of the ten tribute bearers have pronounced negroid features. The gifts include the statue of a lion, a sword, an incense burner, and three Bactrian horses with blankets made of richly decorated brocade. At the end of the scroll is a two-character signature followed by the artist's seal. The title appears in seal characters by Teng Erh-ya, a well-known contemporary collector. The colophon is by Wen Cheng-ming (1470–1559).

Published: d'Argencé, *Asia Foundation*, Pl. XVI (section); *Apollo*, p. 140, Fig. 1 (another section).

114 Landscape in the Manner of Kuo Hsi. Yüan. Anonymous. 14th century A.D.
Hanging scroll. Ink and light colors on silk. H. 42 in., W. 15¾ in. B66D1.

In the foreground is a river scene. In the background towering peaks rise from a misty middle ground where isolated rocks, trees, and the roofs of a temple are buried deep in a valley. The landscape carries a label by Tung Ch'i-ch'ang (1555–1636) and colophons by Weng Fan-kang (dated 1773) and Hsü Yung-hsi (dated 1817).

Published: *Kokka*, No. 584, Pl. 6; d'Argencé, *Asia Foundation*, Fig. 14; *Apollo*, p. 140, Fig. 2.

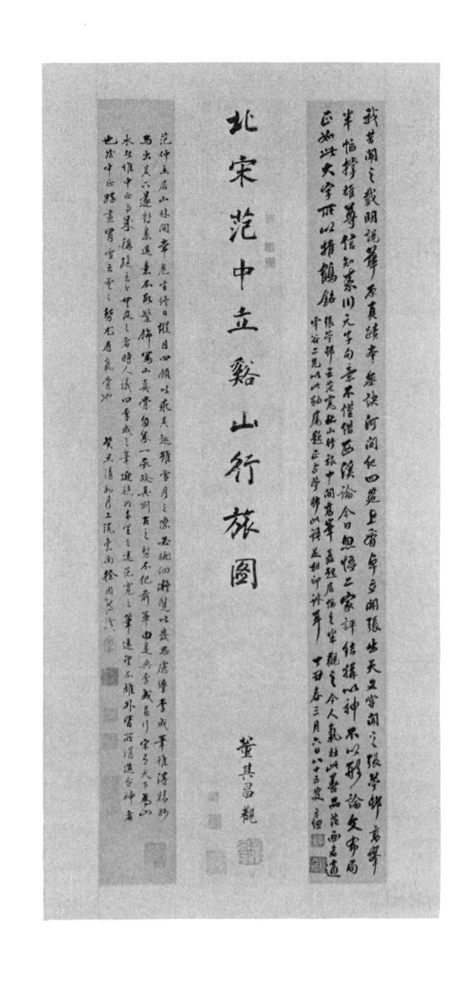

Paintings

115 Brown Landscape. Late Ming.
Tung Ch'i-ch'ang. 1555–1636 A.D.
Hanging scroll. Ink and light colors on silk. H. 56⅓ in., W. 23½ in. B67D1.

The only indication of human life in this "geometric" landscape is the presence of two small cottages in the middle ground. The composition pivots on zigzag water planes. Boulders and trees are uniformly treated in bold, sweeping brushstrokes; many rocky formations are spindle-shaped, and most have a hemp-like quality. The visible sides of the tree branches in the foreground are devoid of foliage. In the upper right corner is a three-line inscription followed by two seals of the artist.

Published: Lee, *Chinese Landscape Painting*, First Ed., Cleveland, 1954, No. 69; J. Cahill, *Chinese Painting*, Geneva, 1960, p. 150.

116 **Landscape.** Early Ch'ing.
K'un-ts'an (active 1650–1675 A.D.)
Dated 1661.
Hanging scroll. Ink on paper. H. 39½ in., W. 47 in. B65D53.

A hamlet in a river bend is sheltered by boulders and desolate cliffs. In the foreground a scholar gazes from the window of a cottage. In the distance are sails on the water and a range of mountains. The whole composition is permeated with unusually firm and rhythmical brush strokes. In a long inscription located in the upper right corner K'un-ts'an, an individualist monk-painter, indulges in detailed and poetic remarks on the privilege of being able to live a secluded life in a remote place where he can keep in close contact with nature. The inscription is preceded and followed by two seals of the artist. In the lower left is a collector's seal.

Published: V. Elisseeff, *Seize Peintures de Maîtres Chinois*, Pl. 9; d'Argencé, *Asia Foundation*, Fig. 15; *Apollo*, p. 141, Fig. 4.

117 **Landscape.** Ch'ing.
Yüan Chiang (active first part of 18th century A.D.).
Dated 1707 A.D.
Hanging scroll. Ink and colors on silk. H. 7 ft., W. 45 in.
B60D85.

In the foreground of this tripartite composition is a rocky promontory projecting into a wide river. The rocks shelter a mansion consisting of several one-story buildings. These architectural elements are rendered in a precise and delicate manner which contrasts vividly with the bold if studied brushwork of the rest of the painting. In the middle ground is seen the opposite bank of the river, with a temple on the extreme left and on the right a hamlet hidden behind a screen of trees. Above, a central towering peak, formed by an accumulation of boulders with very irregular contours, receding far into the distance, emerges from a thick layer of woolly clouds. In the upper left is a two-line inscription followed by two seals of the artist.

丁亥小陽月法劉松年筆意
邗上袁江畫

Key to Abbreviations:

A.B.C. Bronzes:	Lefebvre d'Argencé, René-Yvon, *Ancient Chinese Bronzes in the Avery Brundage Collection.* De Young Museum Society and Diablo Press, San Francisco, 1966.
A.B.C. Ceramics:	Lefebvre d'Argencé, René-Yvon, *Chinese Ceramics in the Avery Brundage Collection.* De Young Museum Society and Diablo Press, San Francisco, 1967.
Apollo:	Vol. LXXXIV, No. 54, London, 1966.
Asia Foundation:	Program Bulletin, Special Issue, San Francisco, 1966.
BMFEA:	Bulletin of the Museum of Far Eastern Antiquities.

Chronology

ca. 2500–1500 B.C.	**Neolithic**				
ca. 1523–1028 B.C.	**Shang**				
ca. 1027–222 B.C.	**Chou**				
	Western Chou	*ca.* 1027–771 B.C.			
	Ch'un-ch'iu	770–481 B.C.			
	Warring States	480–222 B.C.			
221–207 B.C.	**Ch'in**				
206 B.C.–A.D. 220	**Han**				
	Western Han	206 B.C.–A.D. 8			
	Eastern Han	A.D. 25–220			
221–265	**The Three Kingdoms**				
265–589	**The Six Dynasties**				
589–618	**Sui**				
618–906	**T'ang**				
906–960	**The Five Dynasties**				
960–1279	**Sung**				
	Northern Sung	960–1127			
	Southern Sung	1127–1279			
	Liao	907–1125			
	Chin	1115–1234			
1280–1368	**Yüan**				
1368–1644	**Ming**				
	Hung Wu	1368–1398		Chia Ching	1522–1566
	Yung Lo	1403–1424		Lung Ch'ing	1567–1572
	Hsüan Te	1426–1435		Wan Li	1573–1617
	Ch'eng Hua	1465–1467		T'ien Ch'i	1621–1629
	Hung Chih	1488–1505		Ch'ung Chen	1628–1644
	Cheng Te	1506–1521			
1644–1912	**Ch'ing**				
	Shun Chih	1645–1661		Chia Ch'ing	1796–1820
	K'ang Hsi	1662–1722		Tao Kuang	1821–1850
	Yung Cheng	1723–1735		Kuang Hsü	1875–1907
	Ch'ien Lung	1736–1795			

Selected Bibliography

Books and Articles

Cahill, James, *Chinese Painting.* Skira, Geneva, 1960.

Consten, Eleanor von Erdberg, *Das Alte China.* Stuttgart, 1958.

Garner, Sir Harry M., "Sung and Later Ceramic Wares" (in the Avery Brundage Collection), *Apollo*, Vol. LXXXIV, No. 54 (1966), pp. 126–133.

Gyllensvärd, Bo, "The First Floral Patterns on Chinese Bronzes," *BMFEA* (Stockholm), No. 34 (1962), p. 29 ff.

Hochstadter, Walter, "Pottery and Stonewares of Shang, Chou and Han," *BMFEA* (Stockholm), No. 24 (1952), p. 81 ff.

Jenyns, Soame, *Ming Pottery and Porcelain.* Faber and Faber, London, 1953.

Jung Kêng, *Shang and Chou Bronzes.* Harvard-Yenching, Peking, 1944.

Karlgren, Bernhard, "Some Characteristics of the Yin Art," *BMFEA* (Stockholm), No. 34 (1962), p. 1 ff.

Lee, Sherman E., *Chinese Landscape Painting.* Cleveland Museum of Art, Cleveland, 1954.

Lefebvre d'Argencé, René-Yvon, "Early Chinese Ceramics" (in the Avery Brundage Collection), *Apollo*, Vol. LXXXIV, No. 54 (1966), pp. 84–102.

——— "The Magic World of the Chinese Bronze," *Apollo*, Vol. LXXXIV, No. 54 (1966), pp. 113–126.

——— "Chinese Jades from Shang to Ch'ing" (in the Avery Brundage Collection), *Apollo*, Vol. LXXXIV, No. 54 (1966), pp. 134–139.

——— *The Avery Brundage Collection of Asian Art.* Asia Foundation Program Bulletin, Special Issue, San Francisco, 1966.

——— *Ancient Chinese Bronzes in the Avery Brundage Collection.* De Young Museum Society and Diablo Press, San Francisco, 1966.

——— *Chinese Ceramics in the Avery Brundage Collection.* De Young Museum Society and Diablo Press, San Francisco, 1967.

Mizuno, Seiichi, *Bronzes and Jades of Ancient China.* The Nihon Keizei, Tokyo, 1959.

——— *Bronze and Stone Sculpture of China, from Yin to the T'ang Dynasty.* The Nihon Keizai, Tokyo, 1960.

Munsterberg, Hugo, "Chinese Buddhist Bronzes of the T'ang Period," *Artibus Asiae*, XI, 1/2 (1948), pp. 27–45.

Salmony, Alfred, *Chinese Jade through the Wei Dynasty.* The Ronald Press Company, New York, 1963.

Seckel, Dietrich, *The Art of Buddhism.* Crown Publishers, New York, 1964.

Sekino, Tei, *Tenryūzan Sekibutsushū.* Tokyo, 1928.

Sickman, Laurence, and Soper, Alexander, *The Art and Architecture of China.* Penguin Books, London and Baltimore, 1956.

Soper, Alexander, "Chinese Sculptures" (in the Avery Brundage Collection), *Apollo*, Vol. LXXXIV, No. 54 (1966), pp. 103–112.

Trubner, Henry, "Three Important Buddhist Bronzes of the T'ang Dynasty," *Artibus Asiae*, XX, 2/3 (1967), pp. 103–110.

Umehara, Sueji, *Kanan Anyō Ibutsu no Kenkyū (Research on Relics from Anyang, Honan).* Kuwana Bunseidō, Kyoto, 1941.

Watson, William, *Ancient Chinese Bronzes.* Faber and Faber, London, 1962.

Wenley, A. G., "A Hsi Tsun from the Avery Brundage Collection," *ACASA*, Vol. VI (1952), pp. 41–43.

Willetts, William, *Foundations of Chinese Art.* McGraw-Hill, New York, 1965.

Wright, Arthur, *Buddhism in Chinese History.* Stanford University Press, Stanford, California, 1959.

Catalogues of Exhibitions

Elisseeff, Vadime, *Seize Peintures de Maîtres Chinois.* Musée Cernuschi, Paris, 1959.

Hansford, S. Howard, *Exhibition of Chinese Jades.* The Oriental Ceramic Society, London, 1948.

La Plante, John D., *Arts of the Chou Dynasty.* Stanford University Museum, Stanford, California, 1958.

Loo, C. T., *Exhibition of Chinese Arts.* New York, 1941–1942.

Rowland, Benjamin, *The Evolution of the Buddha Image.* The Asia Society, New York, 1963.

Sickman, Laurence, *Selections from the Avery Brundage Collection.* M. H. de Young Memorial Museum, San Francisco, 1960.

Trubner, Henry, *The Arts of the T'ang Dynasty.* Los Angeles, 1957.

Catalogue designed and edited by Virginia Field, Assistant Director, Asia House Gallery.

The following photographs are by William Abbenseth: 2, 3, 4, 5, 6, 7, 8, 9 (color), 11, 12, 13, 14 (color), 15, 16, 18, 20, 21, 24, 25, 28, 29, 31, 32, 33, 34, 46, 47 (color), 48, 53, 54, 56, 58, 61, 62, 64 (color), 65, 68, 72 (color), 73, 77, 78, 81, 82, 85 (color), 87, 96, 97, 98a, 98b, 99 (color), 100 (color), 103 (color), 104, 107, 108, 112, 113, 114, 115 (color), 116, and 117.

The following photographs are by Joe Schopplein: 1, 10, 17, 19, 22, 23, 26, 27, 30, 35, 36, 37, 38, 39, 40, 41, 42, 43, 44, 45, 49, 50, 51, 52, 55, 57, 59, 60, 63, 66, 67, 69, 70, 71, 74, 75, 76, 79, 80, 83, 84, 86, 88, 89, 90, 91, 92, 93, 94, 95, 101, 102, 105, 106, 109, 110, and 111.

Color engravings 9, 64, 74, 85, and 100 courtesy of *Apollo* Magazine.

Color engravings 14, 47, 99, 103, and 113 by Brüder Hartmann, Berlin.

Black-and-white illustrations and text printed by The Meriden Gravure Co., Meriden, Conn.

Composition, color printing, and binding by Clarke & Way, Inc. New York.